CHRIST IS IN OUR MIDST

FATHER JOHN

CHRIST IS IN OUR MIDST

Letters from a Russian Monk

Translated by
Esther Williams

Foreword by
Metropolitan Anthony of Sourozh

ST. VLADIMIR'S SEMINARY PRESS
CRESTWOOD, NEW YORK 10707
1980

First published in Great Britain in 1980
by
DARTON, LONGMAN & TODD LTD.
89 Lillie Road
London SW6 1UD England
and in
The United States of America
by
ST. VLADIMIR'S SEMINARY PRESS
575 Scarsdale Road
Crestwood, New York 10707

Originally published in Russian in *L'Eternel*, Paris, 1961

Library of Congress Cataloging in Publication Data

Ioann, Skhi-igumen, 1873-1958.
Christ is in our midst.

Translation of Pis'ma Valaamskago startsa.
Originally published in the Viechnoe, nos. 1-6 and
8-12, 1961.
Bibliography: p.
Includes index.
1. Ioann, Skhi-igumen, 1873-1958. 2. Orthodox
Eastern Church, Russian—Clergy—Correspondence.
3. Clergy—Russia—Correspondence. I. Title.
BX597.I57I5613   1980   271'.8   80-10530
ISBN 0-913836-64-8

Translation © 1979
THE RUSSIAN ORTHODOX DIOCESE OF SOUROZH
34 Upper Addison Gardens
London W14, England

ISBN 0-913836-64-8

PRINTED IN THE UNITED STATES OF AMERICA
BY
ATHENS PRINTING COMPANY
461 Eighth Avenue
New York, NY 10001

CONTENTS

BIOGRAPHICAL NOTE CONCERNING FATHER JOHN

In 1873 Ivan Alekseyevich Alekseyev was born to a good peasant couple living in a Tver village north of Moscow. After a simple education learned from visitors to his home, the young Ivan began searching for a monastery in which to live a life dedicated to God. At sixteen he entered Valamo Monastery. After four years at Valamo he had to leave to fulfil his four years' term of military service in a rifle battalion. He then lived again with his family for a couple of years before returning to Valamo Monastery in 1900. Seven years later he became a member of the brotherhood; in 1910 he was accepted as a monk, being given the name Yakinf (Hyacynthos – the Greek martyr). During the next eleven years he served in various capacities at the main monastery at Valamo, in the hermitages of the prophet Elijah and of St Herman as well as in Valamo's filial monastery in Petrograd.

In 1921 within a period of two weeks, monk Yakinf was ordained monk-deacon, then priest-monk, and sent to serve as Superior at St Tryphon Monastery in Petsamo on the Arctic coast. Eleven years later, at his own request, he returned to Valamo to head a small monastic community living on John the Baptist island. There he was consecrated to the great schema and was named John.

In 1938, on the eve of the Finnish-Russian winter war, schema-monk John was chosen by the monks to be their Father Confessor. During the war the famous old monastery at Valamo had to be hastily abandoned. The monks established a modest New Valamo at Heinävesi in Finland where schema-monk John lived until he died peacefully in his cell in 1958. New Valamo still has a few Russian monks living in it but is now becoming a Finnish-speaking community.

(Based on an introduction by Tito Colliander to the Finnish translation published by Werner Söderström in 1976.)

TRANSLATOR'S INTRODUCTORY NOTE

A staretz is a monk singled out because of his saintliness, spiritual experience and ability to guide the souls of others. The startsi have maintained the tradition in the Eastern Church of the unceasing prayer of the heart known as the Jesus Prayer. Through many centuries the Fathers and ascetics have given guidance to those seeking the Kingdom, and their writings have been an invaluable guide to succeeding generations. A unique collection of such writings is contained in the five volumes of the *Philokalia*, to which we find constant reference in the letters of Father John. The *Philokalia* has not been translated into English in its entirety, but the work is going on, and many of the writings referred to by Father John can be found in English. Chapter and page references to these translations have been added to the text in square brackets or referred to in footnotes relating to the bibliography on p. 147. Biblical references have also been added to the text in square brackets. All of the footnotes are the translator's. Where no translation exists, references are to the Russian text.

These letters, sent by Father John to many of his spiritual

children, were collected and sent to Paris for publication in Russian in the journal *L'Eternel* in 1961. They were reprinted in Finland in 1976 and in the same year a translation into Finnish by Archbishop Paavali was published. In the present English translation from the Russian the order of the letters has been altered somewhat to make it more strictly chronological. The first two letters were written from the old Valamo Monastery situated on islands in Lake Ladoga near the Finnish–Russian border.

I wish to express my gratitude to Mrs Pegeen O'Sullivan, who checked the translation and made many valuable suggestions.

FOREWORD:
WHEN A MAN STARTS ON THE WAY

True conversion, repentance, and rejection of evil are the very substance of the Christian life. One who pronounces monastic vows seems to do no more than renew the vows of baptism; yet there is more to it. He undertakes to live the rest of his life as though he had already died, being a stranger not only to sin but also to compromise. 'Carrying in his body the death of Christ' means renouncing himself radically and ruthlessly, so that only the will of God as expressed in the Holy Gospel and revealed to him in holy obedience may mould and re-create him 'after the image of Him who created him'. He is to cling to the Truth, walk along the path of the commandments and be yoked together with Christ not only to the extent of taking up his own cross, but also, like Simon of Cyrene, of participating in the carrying of Christ's own Cross. He wants to know no other way but Christ. He seeks to cling to all that is good and to turn away from all that is evil.

At the end and summit of the monastic life, however, there is another step which few are allowed to take: to let go of the very notions of good and evil; to let go even of doing good; and to know nothing but God in a final, ultimate surrender, in the wisdom of holy ignorance, in the simplicity of a return to the spirit of childhood which aims at nothing, plans nothing, but responds at once without reservation to all Divine promptings. St Seraphim was asked how it was that he knew what to say to every person at first sight. He replied that he knew nothing but said what came to his mind, unquestioningly, as coming from the deep serenity of God's own presence. When the staretz Silouan was asked: 'How do the saints speak?' he answered: 'By the Spirit of God', 'by the Holy Spirit'. All this seems baffling: it is so offensively simple and direct. Yet this is 'mere Christianity' – so alien and strange to the modern sophisticated mind which has lost touch with the heart, the core of man's being, the depth where we can find God's holy dwelling-place.

The writings of Staretz John will strike many a reader as being 'too simple', 'too primitive', naïve, perhaps even trivial. Many of his letters refer to the most ordinary things of life, such as receiving a damaged parcel or getting news. However, from all the circumstances of life he draws lessons that connect them with Life. With the wisdom of a heart open to God he discerns in all of them a depth, a significance, a dimension of eternity. An old Russian priest once said in a sermon: 'Only the Holy Spirit can make us see the eternal significance of things too trivial for us'.

Read these letters as though they were written to you personally. When you are on the point of saying, 'But he has already said that several times', ask yourself, 'And what have I done about it?' If it seems to you that something is really too small to be put into the context of God, remember Christ's own saying that not a hair falls from your head without the Father being aware of it. If you feel too worldly wise to have anything to learn from such a simpleton, ask yourself how much you know of the deep things of God experientially – not in your intellect, but in your deepest self, at the core of your being – and what use it is to you to know so many things, while you do so little.

St Arsenius of Egypt, who had been the preceptor of the children of a Roman emperor and a man celebrated for his learning, left the court, retired to the desert and became the disciple of an illiterate ascetic. 'How can you submit to the guidance of such an ignoramus?' exclaimed some of his former acquaintances. 'He can already read a book the letters of which I cannot yet spell', was the reply.

May God bless you with humble wisdom, with a silent and receptive heart, and may the prayers of Father John bring you to that simplicity which allows one to see.

Metropolitan Anthony of Sourozh
London, 14 May 1979

PREFACE

New Valamo, 5 February 1956

My beloved children!

You have collected my letters and would like to publish them. You know I wrote the letters at different times and to different people, so they are inevitably repetitious. It would be good if I could read them again, but this is impossible as my ailing legs prevent me from coming to you. I am certainly getting decrepit. I am already eighty-three years old. I thank God that my memory, although it grows dull, has not failed me.

I wrote the letters as the Lord laid it upon my heart. I am a man of shy nature and limited mind – of this I am fully aware – and my memory is poor. I have not been to school and I wrote just as I speak.

In those days there was still no kerosene; at night people worked in their huts by the light of a splinter.[1] I looked after the fire, always putting a new splinter into the holder, and the embers fell into a ready bucket of water. My father

1. Wood dipped in tallow and used as a torch.

plaited bast[2] shoes, and my mother and sisters spun or mended. I also had two brothers. And this is interesting: matches did not exist; a hollow was made in the stove, the glowing coals were raked into it with a coal-rake and in that way a fire was kept alive. If it happened that the coals went out, mother would say: 'Vanka, go down to Andrew's for coals'. And so I brought coals in a little pot. I blew on the coals, lit a splinter – and there we had light again!

A tailor came to us to make fur coats. He could read, and he began teaching me. I was a dull learner, but my sister learned the letters quickly and reproached me, 'How is it you can't understand? I have learned already, and you still don't understand!' At last I too learned to read.

When I had begun reading I acquired a few booklets of *Lives of Saints* – at that time such booklets were printed. I had a friend of like mind. We pondered together how to be saved. We went on foot to the Nil Hermitage 15 kilometres away. We dried some rusks, put them in a knapsack and off we went. We walked there this way three times. We had heard that a hermitess Matrona was living there in the woods, but we found no way of meeting her. Of course we were rather stupid: we were only thirteen years old.

My eldest brother lived in Petrograd. He was good at business and not stupid; he had an eating-house and he took me in. I lived with him a little while and acquired more booklets all the time. Once when my brother went to the country I went to Konevitsa Monastery. A travelling companion who knew Finnish turned up. We did not like

2. Flexible tree bark.

Konevitsa, so we went on to Valamo. I stayed at Valamo, but my companion went back to Petrograd. I was then sixteen. My mother came to visit me. When I had spent four years in the monastery I was called up for military service. I served in the rifle battalion for four years – that was the term of service in those days. After my service I lived for a couple of years at my father's and then for the second time came to Valamo in 1900. I have been living in a monastery ever since and it has never entered my mind to return to the world.

I thank the Lord that in his mercy He granted me, sinner that I am, to spend my whole life in a monastery. Whoever reads my letters, I fervently beg him: remember this great sinner in your holy prayers.

A staretz of Valamo Monastery

I received your esteemed letter and I see from it that you have begun to take an interest in the inner spiritual life. May the Lord give you wisdom! You are right in saying that we should not expect anything from prayer. In prayer one should keep a sense of being very unworthy and if warmth and tears come, one should not think highly of oneself; let them come and go without any coercion, but do not be troubled when they disappear: it cannot be otherwise.

Prayer is the most difficult of spiritual exercises, and to our last breath it involves the labour of hard struggle. Yet the Lord in his mercy also gives comfort at times to the one who prays, so that he may not weaken. Set your own rule for private prayer according to the time available; there will be no arbitrariness in this. But I advise you not to take on much, so as not to be a slave to the rule, and in order to avoid haste.

By God's mercy all is well here for the present. We are living the usual monastic life.

May God bless you.

It is good that you are practising the Jesus Prayer. The Holy Fathers called prayer the queen of virtues, for it attracts other virtues too. But the higher it is, the more work it requires. St Agathon says: 'Prayer is warfare to the last breath'.

You say the prayer one hundred times morning and evening. That is enough for you, only try to do it with attention. Do not be disconcerted when your heart is dry in prayer; press on anyway, only keep your attention, as I told you, on the upper part of your chest. At work and with people try to stand with your mind before God, that is remember God, that He is present. If psalms and akathists[3] move you most, read them if there is time.

We do not dare to ask the Lord for unceasing prayer of the mind in the heart, which you are striving for – it is a very rare state which hardly one in a thousand people attain, according to Isaac the Syrian, and this spiritual degree is reached by the grace of God and through deep humility. Do not strive for warmth of heart – it comes without our seeking and waiting for it. In prayer our part should be to work, but success depends on grace; seek nothing more and do not get excited. In the spiritual life there is no place for leaps; what is required is patience. You are still young in both body and spirit. St John of the Ladder writes: 'Open the soul of a beginner and you will find error. He wants to have unceasing prayer, constant

3. Services consisting of songs of praise.

memory of death and perfect freedom from anger, but only the perfect are in that state.' The mark of prayer is in warmth and contrition of heart, and in recognizing one's nothingness, and calling to the Lord: 'Lord, Jesus Christ, Son of God, have mercy on me, a sinner',[4] or you can pray with other words as it suits you best.

You do not want to sin, yet you sin gravely. What can you do? We are human beings, bearers of flesh, and are tempted by devils. Do not tremble and do not be depressed like that, even when a virtue is tottering. Stand up, straighten yourself and go forward again. Know that stability in virtue depends not on us, but on the grace of God. Have humility and do not trust yourself until you reach the grave, nor condemn others for anything. Anyone who condemns another falls into the same sins himself. It is never otherwise.

If you sometimes have to use a little deception in order to stay at home for the sake of your soul's solitude, it is not sinful; see to it that everything is for God's sake. May the Lord give you wisdom.

3   *27 April 1940*

I received your letter. By God's mercy I am still alive. Although I sleep on a plank-bed I am peaceful in spirit and do not even think about Valamo – just as if I had not lived there.

4. This prayer, of long tradition in the Church, is called the Jesus Prayer.

I understood your letter, for it was written from your feelings and I felt the force of the words. I left Valamo in peace, and had stood the bombardment of Valamo with equanimity. During the alarm I did not run and hide in the bomb shelter although it was in our main church, but I sat in my cell and read the Holy Gospel. The thunder of bombs shook the building, window-panes were shattered to bits and doors flew open, but I had an inner conviction that I would stay alive. We had to leave Valamo hurriedly. Although we could take little with us, I have no regret about that, but it is a great pity that your icon, and also the one given to me with my parents' blessing, were left hanging on the wall. I took a few books of the Holy Fathers, and that is enough.

Although you have been freed from passions, have humility and do not trust yourself until you reach the grave. It is our task to work for every virtue, but success depends on the grace of God, and God awards his grace not for work but for humility. In so far as a person humbles himself, he is visited by grace. I advise you to read St Makarios the Great, his five talks on purity of heart. They were printed there at your place.

4   *27 July 1940*

Your state is a blessed one if you feel small and like a child among spiritually mature people. Do not envy such people and do not strive for spiritual raptures. Mystics strive for such feelings of grace, and instead of reaching true contemplation they fall into diabolic self-deception. The Lord grants to a man a sense of grace if his heart is purified of passions. The Holy Fathers were in such a state, but we sinners ought to pray with penitence and ask for God's help in our struggle with passions. The *Paterikon*[5] tells how a disciple said to a staretz that such-and-such a man 'sees angels'. The staretz answered: 'This is not surprising, that he sees angels, but I would marvel at a person who saw his own sins'. Brief as this saying of the staretz is, its spiritual meaning is very deep, because nothing is so difficult as to know oneself. You write: 'The words of the prayer and the Lord have united and are, as it were, inseparably the Lord himself'. There is no mistake here. So it should be.

Yes, 'ease, wealth, parental love and being praised by people' are a great hindrance in the spiritual life. The Holy Fathers greatly feared these causes of sin and avoided them with all their might. It was no mistake that they went off to monasteries and deserts, but you do not need to run anywhere. Just try to be wise as a serpent and innocent as a dove. All else is transitory, empty, like tinsel. One must remember and even convince oneself that if we do not die today, we shall tomorrow, and there we face eternal life, and time stands still. Lord have mercy.

Your age and your path are very slippery. Be humble and do not trust yourself until you are in your grave. May the Lord give you wisdom!

Go on praying as you are now. If you have the *Lives of*

5. A collection of sayings of the Fathers.

5

the Saints I would advise you to read them now and then. They are very inspiring and have much to teach.

With love in Christ.

5   *Undated*

Thank God for letting you have even a little taste that 'God is good'. It is true that one should not reveal one's inner state even to a confessor if he is not living the same kind of inner life. St Anthony the Great writes: 'If you speak about a spiritual matter to one who is not spiritual, it will seem ridiculous to him'. In the letter before last I wrote to you about humility, and I repeat once more: Be humble, my child, the enemy is very cunning and we are very weak. St Makarios writes: 'I have known people who were in such a state of spiritual perfection that they saw the glory of the saints in heaven and were in that state for six years, and yet – dreadful to say – they perished'.[6] He also refers to some martyrs who endured severe tortures but later fell. About the forgiveness of sins, the Holy Spirit speaks through the prophet Ezekiel, saying: 'If a sinner repents and lives a good life, the Lord does not remember his sins'. And likewise, if a righteous man becomes corrupted, the Lord does not remember his righteousness [Ezek. 18:21–4].

Try to discriminate, my child. Be wise as a serpent and innocent as a dove.

This living in a common room and sleeping side by side on boards is very good for me. God is one, but the paths

6. See Homily 27,14.

that lead to Him are many. We see this in the example of the Holy Fathers: some of them practised inner prayer of the mind and prospered in the spiritual life, while others read many psalms, canons and troparions[7] and also prospered in the spiritual life. Let me add: the Holy Fathers write that even in the saints, natural shortcomings remain – for the sake of humility.

To be on Tabor with the Saviour is a very joyous thing, but when you have to be at Golgotha be patient – you have ears to hear; listen, be attentive.

May the Lord give you wisdom!

6   *14 September 1943*

Christ is in our midst!

It helps little if we only read and ask how to be saved. We must exert ourselves, work, and purify our hearts from passions. You know now what spiritual life is. Now is the time, begin, may the Lord teach you, and do not forget me in your holy prayers.

Yes, Holy Father Isaac's language is difficult, but it is still more difficult for us to understand the content, for the well is deep and our rope is short and we cannot reach his deep, wonderful, saving water.

Bishop Theophan even made a special prayer to St Isaac asking him to help us understand his saving teaching. In general the Holy Fathers wrote from their experience and

7. Canon: a liturgical form based on nine scriptural songs. Troparions are stanzas of religious poetry.

feelings, and their teaching is understood by those who are working on their own hearts.

May God bless you!

7   *14 August 1945*

Christ is in our midst!.

I received your esteemed letter and read it with love.

It is good that you aspire to the spiritual life, but try not to quench the spirit. Even though it is harder for you to develop the spiritual life in the world, the Lord helps those who try.

St John of the Ladder wonders at our strange condition: why is it that although we have the all-powerful God and the angels and holy people to help us do good, and only the crafty evil spirit to help us to sin, still we are more readily and easily moved to passions and vices than to virtue? The question was left open. The saint did not want to explain it to us. However, one can guess that our nature, corrupted by disobedience, and the world with its various stupefying temptations are helping the devil, and the Lord does not infringe upon our sovereign will. We should strive for virtue to the limit of our strength, but to stand firm in virtue is not in our power but in the Lord's. The Lord preserves us in virtue in response not to our labours but to our humility. Where there has been a fall, it has been preceded by pride, says John of the Ladder.[8]

8. John Climacus, author of *The Ladder of Divine Ascent.*

But the Lord in his mercy has given penitence to us feeble ones, since our corrupted nature is so very prone to sin. The Holy Fathers from their own experience have studied minutely the subtleties of our nature and they console us, offering detailed writings on ways to combat sin. You now have the book *Unseen Warfare*: consult it more often.

With regard to your rule of prayer, arrange it yourself, but in such a way that meaning is not lost for the sake of completing the rule. Try to pray attentively. Is it not better to shorten it than to complete it in agitation and be a slave to the rule? This is not my idea, but that of Isaac the Syrian. It is also said in *Unseen Warfare*, I do not remember in which chapter.

Your unworthy companion in prayer.

8   *11 February 1946*

Highly esteemed in the Lord!

By God's mercy I am well; after dinner I go to saw wood for a couple of hours. Do not be frightened about your lack of devotion in prayer: it is a good and saving thing that you force yourself to pray; look at the *Ladder*, 28:29. ['Do not say, after spending a long time at prayer, that nothing has been gained; for you have already gained something. And what higher good is there than to cling to the Lord and persevere in unceasing union with him?']

Do not imagine God to be very severe. He is very gracious and knows our human weaknesses. We must rever-

ently venerate the Holy Fathers, for they are specially chosen by God, but if it troubles you that we are unable to
imitate them, see what the *Ladder* 26:125 says. ['The man
who despairs of himself when he hears of the supernatural
virtues of the saints is most unreasonable. On the contrary,
they teach you supremely one of two things: either they
rouse you to emulation by their holy courage, or they lead
you by way of thrice-holy humility to deep self-knowledge
and realization of your inherent weakness.']

I too desire that the Lord should count you worthy to
spend the end of your life in a convent. Let us hope and
pray that He will fulfil our desire. In the meantime, live
with N and serve her in accordance with the fifth commandment ['Honour your father and your mother' . . .].
For the monastic life store up patience, not a cartload of it,
but a train of carts.

I do not like my illiterate letters, so I wrote that you
should destroy them, but if in your humility you want to
keep them, let them remain with you. Write to me, don't
restrain yourself. I shall always answer as far as the Lord
gives me understanding. Sometimes I am disturbed by the
thought: 'Why do I, unlettered as I am, carry on correspondence with educated people?' Let us hope that God will
grant us to meet, and then we will talk. The writings of the
Holy Fathers are addressed to three degrees of spiritual
perfection: infants, those in progress, and the perfect. Since
you and I are babes, we need and can use soft food, so take
from the spiritual writings what is suited to your age.

The Lord give you understanding; sort yourself out and
do not be troubled.

We have entered the holy forty days' fast. The Holy Church sings: 'Let us keep a fast pleasing and acceptable to the Lord. A true fast is alienation from evils; restraint of the tongue; laying aside of anger; giving up of lusts, false accusations and perjury – lack of these things is a true and acceptable fast'.

On Forgiveness Sunday after supper there was half an hour's break and at seven o'clock all the monks gathered in the church. They sang the Easter canon and read the evening prayers, after which they kissed the icons. The Igumen[9] asked forgiveness and bowed to the ground and likewise the whole brotherhood bowed to the ground in front of him and each in turn came to ask forgiveness of him and one another, kissing one another on the shoulders. All the time one could hear: 'May God forgive you; forgive me, a sinner'. Then in silence they dispersed to their cells.

What a good custom; it somehow seems to speak to the soul very well. All were reconciled. This whole week there is no work; there will be Communion on Saturday.

Lenten greetings to you; the Lord help you to spend the fast in Christian piety and to meet Christ's Bright Resurrection.

9. Title used in Russian and Greek for the Superior of a monastic community.

Christ is in our midst!

My wish for you is that you should lead a spiritual life and try to express all that is in your soul for God's sake for the salvation of your soul. 'Take heed lest you fall', says the Apostle [1 Cor. 10:12]. Yet without God's grace all our precautions come to naught, for it is not in our power to hold to virtues, as I have said to you before. What is within our free will is to compel ourselves to press firmly towards virtue.

You now have an understanding of the inner life and some experience as well; make yourself pray inwardly more often as far as you have, strength and time. Also practise remembrance of death and pray to God to give you this memory. Observe what our temporal life is like: inconstant, changeable, and quickly passing, distracting inattentive people so that they become scattered. But there is one means for gaining inner peace, and that is unceasing prayer. Boredom and dejection will pass; be patient, do not be despondent; the Lord will help and keep you.

It is not right to believe what you hear from outsiders. People being what they are, they sometimes make mountains out of mole-hills and see only weaknesses. They cannot see the tears shed in the monk's cell, nor can they penetrate the inner life of a solitary monk. The stages of spiritual progress vary and it takes a spiritual man to recognise a spiritual man. The most profitable thing is to see all people as good and oneself as the worst of all. Just observe yourself and you will see yourself worse than anyone. I did tell you this before, in a personal conversation.

I always remember you in my unworthy prayers, and may God's mercy be with you according to your faith.

11   *24 October 1946*

Heartfelt thanks for the trouble you took. Praise and thanks to God that the Lord helped you to be peaceful with N. The Lord help her; we must not judge her. The book by St Isaac the Syrian is very deep; it can be understood accurately only by people leading a spiritual life. If you can get hold of the book by Cassian of Rome, I advise you to read it – particularly his Conferences, because you have begun a little to understand the thoughts of the Holy Fathers. It is good that you sometimes discuss the inner life; what you know – you can explain.

You expressed curiosity about the kind of voice the Saviour had. He was perfect God and perfect man, but without sin; one must suppose that He spoke like a man. But his speech had no typically human, artificial eloquence; rather it was filled with greatness. And when He unmasked the Pharisees, He must have spoken sternly.

The Lord keep you!

12   *15 November 1946*

By God's mercy I am perfectly well and do not need to go to doctors. My work is not difficult: I go to work after dinner for about two and a half hours to collect sticks in the forest and pile them up. This is good for both body and soul.

You and N are different and that is why your heart is not drawn towards her. God is one, but the paths leading to Him are different and each goes his own way.

Thanks to N for the child's prayer. A child's prayer is quick to reach God. I remember well her singing and the story of the holy priest. Children have a special quality of simplicity, candour and naturalness; the Lord commanded us to be like that. All the ascetics have had that quality.

If you observe yourself sharply you will really see that you are worse than anyone. Then you will not even be harmed by anyone's praise. For people only look at the outside of a man and they do not know what is inside – except those who are leading a spiritual life.

Prayer requires a struggle until the very hour of death. It is good that you are striving for prayer. The Lord help you; do not quench the spirit.

13   *4 December 1946*

It was very nice to visit you. However, my years remind me that the candle of my life is already burning low; it will soon go out – just send up a little smoke and vanish altogether. We should remember that this life of ours passes very quickly and that it is a preparation for the future eternal life. If we do not see one another here, I believe we shall in the future life, for you and I are united not bodily but spiritually.

I received your parcels sent with the nun N and Father X. The pies were each more delicious than the other and sweeter than any bakery pies, for love and labour make sweet. Please do not send me anything in future. We have everything provided here, but there you have to provide everything for yourselves. The Lord help you.

Read the book of Makarios the Great carefully, because he speaks very deeply about the spiritual life. His writing can be called an inspection of the spiritual life. If you search round in your heart you will find there a hundred-headed dragon. However, do not be afraid and do not quail: with God's help you will crush its heads. When you watch your life you will see that you are very bad and weak and you will not judge others but will see everyone to be good. You will not even pay attention to others' weaknesses and you will feel stillness and peace in your heart. At times comforting tears will appear.

Today is the feast of the Entry of the Holy Mother of God into the Temple. We had an impressive ceremony with singing in two choirs. The weather is fine; the sun is shining. It is irresistible. I shall go for a walk. I like walking alone; I love nature. Wherever I look, everything comforts me: every tree and bush, and the little birds twittering as they fly from tree to tree and clasp the twigs with their little feet and carry something in their bill; a white hare runs past, stands up on her hind legs, listens, looks from side to side and hops on. All this is so instructive, one cannot help crying, and in everything God's Providence is visible. How marvellously everything is created and how graciously He takes care of everything; with Him nothing is forgotten. The birds are so small, their legs like little match-sticks, and they manage to live and find food in the cold season! Glory to thy wisdom, O Lord, glory to thy creation! I thank Thee, Lord, that we with our many sins and weaknesses are sometimes granted entry to knowledge of Thee; this is thy mercy. Without thy help we sinners cannot contemplate nature nor acquire a single virtue. Our free will which Thou hast given can only strive towards virtue, but to attain it or persevere in it depends on thy help. I ask Thee one thing, Lord: order our lives, save us sinners.

14   *6 December 1946*

It would be good to have a personal talk with you about the questions you raise, because it is not possible to say everything in a letter. It has to be like that when a person examines himself; then other people appear to be good, for a straight eye sees everything straight and a crooked eye sees everything crooked. So you have now got a copy of St Cassian's book. Read a bit of it. Although it is addressed to monks, it applies to laymen too. Some well-selected extracts from this book are included in the second volume of the *Philokalia*. You like reading the lives of saints – do read them, they are very inspiring for us sinners. Here they are read every day at meals, and I have noticed tears come to the eyes of some.

So you yourself have noticed that visitors and conversations leave you depressed. Do avoid them as far as possible, without a qualm. People may be a little displeased, but never mind; do not let that bother you. You say you are afraid of the dark. So am I. That shows how weak we are and how little faith we have in God's providence. Once when I was coming back from the nuns on foot and had to walk five kilometres through the forest in the dark, at one place I was seized with such fear that my whole body was as if crawling with ants and my ears began to move; it felt as if someone was coming after me. I turned round, made the sign of the Cross and went on. Holy Scripture says: 'Fear is nothing other than the abandonment of reason' [Wisdom of Solomon 17:11]'.

As to your confusion, the Holy Fathers said: 'Anything that has to do with confusion comes from the demons'. Kiss the Cross and the icon of the Mother of God and that is enough, be at peace. Look in St Barsanuphius at the 430th question and answer, as well as the 433rd question and answer; there you can clarify things a little for yourself.

Never mind if you do not always manage to complete your whole rule: do not be a slave to the rule. Keep the rule of the publican: 'God be merciful to me, a sinner' and remember God; this takes the place of every rule. Read page 136 [ch. 53,256f] of St Isaac's book and chapter twenty in part two of *Unseen Warfare*. When tears come, stop and wait until they are over. Tears are always helpful; do not be troubled about them. Realize that praying without attentiveness would never bring tears.

17

When you go to bed let God be in your thoughts: something you remember from Holy Scripture, especially from the Gospels. Let any tears come freely.

In confession do not try to have tears. Say what is on your conscience, nothing more. Obviously N is going through a hard situation and it is necessary to pray for her and not be angry with her. Yes you are right not to pay attention to her or interfere. The Lord give you wisdom and reconciliation.

15   *1946*

I received your note from the sanatorium. I see from it that your spirit faints within you and your heart is appalled and you feel out of joint and good for nothing, and now you are surprised at yourself. You did not notice that in a subtle way you were self-satisfied and thought you were already flying to heaven, whereas you lacked true inner humility and perfect surrender to God's will. The Lord in his compassion sent a change into your usual life, and you fell in spirit and felt good for nothing. Yet this is just what humility is, to feel good for nothing.

Do not be depressed, my child; force yourself to pray and by God's mercy all that muddy slough which rose up within you will settle down and there will be stillness and peace. I advise you not to hurry to leave the sanatorium. Have a good rest. The Lord help and keep you.

You write that I have undertaken to teach you sense. But it is not so: how can I teach others when I myself am groping and stumbling? If a blind person leads a blind person, both will fall into the pit. From your long correspondence with N you probably still have his letters and remember his advice. How could I, ignorant as I am, guide others in such a great matter, which is more precious than all the world? I have not got spiritual experience of my own, and if I give someone an answer which is not my own but borrowed from the Holy Fathers, it makes me blush: I teach others, and myself, how do I live?

In our time we are not blessed with the possibility of living under the guidance of a staretz experienced in the spiritual life. A guide should show the way he himself has gone. If he only guides according to the books, it is quite a different thing. The speaker and the listener think that they are both being edified, but when they taste how good is the Lord they recognize their mistakes. St Peter the Damascene says of himself: 'I suffered a great deal of harm from inexperienced advisers'. A guide should be free of passions and have the gift of good judgement, which means: to know the right time; how to begin; how to proceed; what is the structure of a man, his strength, knowledge, zeal, maturity, capacity for warmth, his constitution, health and sickness, morality, place, education, disposition, purpose, conduct, understanding, native intellect, endeavour, courage, sluggishness; what is God's purpose, the meaning of each saying of Divine Scripture and much else. This is what a spiritual guide must be and what judgement he must have.

To my shame I have lived in a monastery forty-eight years already and am in such disarray that I simply do not know where to begin, how to save my soul. Do not think that I speak this way out of humility. No, no, it is truly so. In my youth I had more than enough zeal. For some time I wore a hair shirt and fetters. I tried to find holy ascetic men, but somehow was not successful. Probably I could not understand them because of my inexperience. The initial fervour makes one give a great deal of attention to the letter which kills the spirit, and I did not meet a teacher who could support my zeal and give me proper spiritual guidance. Yet a person who lives without guidance – according to John of the Ladder [26,72.] – is 'unreliable', for he gets puffed up. So I was left with nothing. But I do not lose hope; I believe in God's mercy and strive towards Him according to my strength. I remember the vineyard in the Gospel [Matt. 20], in which hirelings came even at the eleventh hour and received the same pay as those who had worked since morning. I am very content and glad that the Lord ordained that I should spend my life within the walls of a monastery.

You wrote that you 'love good food'; who does not? Only he who has tasted heavenly consolation and restrains his belly – that lord of all evil.

I wrote that the letter kills the spirit, but the purpose of the words must be rightly understood: the letter kills those who stop there and see it as a virtue and not as a means towards virtue. Of course there are no fruits without leaves. However, the fig tree withered without fruits.

I remain with love in Christ.

17   *21 February 1947*

I congratulate you and N on the beginning of Lent. The Lord help you to spend it in a way pleasing to Him and to reach the bright feast of the Resurrection of Christ.

Now you have the book by St Barsanuphius: glance into it – it is very instructive. You can find in the index the questions that deal with the things which puzzle you. I am sending you a small book to read which presents systematically the moral teaching of Isaac the Syrian; read it unhurriedly.

Father N's spiritual daughter does not write to me. I am glad of that, for I would not like to make many acquaintances. But you, write to me when you feel like it and with love I will answer as far as I am able. I want you to be a true Christian in the full sense. Smoking, of course, is not good, but I am more strict about passions of the soul: envy, rancour, arrogance, slyness, hypocrisy, flattery and greed for money. But the bodily passions are sometimes very humbling. The worst thing is pride, for it was by pride that the devil turned his brightness to darkness. Pride is the invention of the devil. When we meet, God willing, let us talk about the passions of the soul.

Strive for humility, my child, and do not trust yourself this side of the grave. It is not in our power to hold to virtue; that is a matter of grace, and grace works only through humility. John of the Ladder says: 'Where a fall has overtaken us, pride has already pitched its tent'. It is a great good fortune for us to have the books of the Holy Fathers, for they speak in detail about the spiritual life. Of course it would be good to lead a spiritual life under the guidance of a spiritual director, but holy men have become fewer, and without a director it is very dangerous to be guided only by books, just in the way that a person who has not studied medicine can go to the pharmacy and choose something poisonous instead of useful medicines. However, we must not despair. Let us make the publican's humility our foundation and the Lord in his goodness will help us sinners and deliver us from disasters on the spiritual path. And let us repent of our weaknesses, for all the wrestlers for piety have held to humility and penitence.

The great staretz Paissy Velichkovsky also grieved that there were no guides, but on the basis of his experience in the spiritual life he advised simply consulting with like-minded people, discussing and reading together the books of the Holy Fathers. So your group is very useful, for you exchange ideas there. You need not be worried when there are differences of opinion: this happens even among the spiritual wrestlers. God is one, and people come to Him from different directions. So it is very precious and useful to have a like-minded person to talk with. St Seraphim said: 'If you want to put yourself into disorder, talk with a man of another turn of mind', and experience shows this to be true. Sometimes speaking with one person is simply a rest, while speaking with another is heavy; it is close to a quarrel; there is little to say; one is thinking how to get away as soon as possible.

You have the second volume of the *Philokalia*; read St Hesychios on sobriety and prayer. The struggle with thoughts is very well presented. I often look at it; it is hard to tear myself away from it and I never get tired of reading it. It is very inspiring; even though we do not follow its advice it is still useful to know what is the essence of the spiritual life.

What a long letter I have written, and not very coherent, but never mind.

The Lord keep you!

18   *2 March 1947*

Christ is in our midst!

You write that you are not stable, and so it is, you are like a reed shaken by the wind. When a breeze of news blew, you began to sway to and fro. And the reasons are these: distraction and inattention to your inner life, and weakness of resolve to follow God's will. As soon as you hear praise of your homeland you are ready to go there. But you must realize that wherever you go, you will carry your inner chaos with you. There too you will meet people, not angels, and the Kingdom of God is not outside us, but within.

If we see to the one thing needful, then all the rest will be added, for this was said by the Lord Himself.

Today is Sunday (the Feast of Orthodoxy). A week of

the fast has already gone, time is flying as if on wings. How short is this earthly life of ours in comparison to the eternal life to come – like a grain of sand in the sea. And yet we give so little thought to eternity and prepare ourselves poorly for it. Indeed we have made ourselves very worldly and have forgotten to ponder the one thing needful. Lord, give me remembrance of death.

19   *29 April 1947*

I received your letter, and although you wrote it on the train I could make out everything.

Although it is painful to our self-conceit to listen to gossip, we must endure it patiently and ask for God's help, for without God's help we cannot succeed in any virtue. I always repeat this to you, for it is true.

In reading the book *In the Caucasian Mountains** omit from the middle of page xi to the middle of page xvii, as well as the third and fourth chapters. In those places mistakes have crept in. The enemy influenced the author in order to undermine the readers' confidence. Read it with trust, it is a very useful book. I often have a glance at it, for one can see that it was written not with the mind but with feeling and with the taste of the spiritual fruits of the one thing needful.

Warm greetings, my child.

* See note on page 149.

24

About your anxiety and stumbling I will say this: as long
as the ship of our soul is sailing on the sea of life it will
always be subject to changes of weather: now rain, now
fine weather. Sometimes a storm blows up and it looks as
if the boat were about to strike a reef or run aground. It
cannot be otherwise in this vale of tears. Only in the life to
come will changes cease. When we are subject to passions
– I mean those of the soul, such as conceit, vanity, anger,
slyness and demonic pride – under the influence of these
passions we think that all people are blameworthy and no
good. However, we have not been commanded to require
love and justice from others, but it is our own duty to fulfil
the commandments of love and to be just. But do not be
depressed. In times of trouble go deep into Holy Scriptures
and the Holy Fathers and into prayer. Then you will experience peace and quiet in your soul. By our own reason, no
matter how hard we think, without God's help we cannot
be reconciled with ourselves or bring peace to others.

The Lord keep you.

21   *15 July 1947*

I received the herring; you even took the trouble to take
out the bones. Thank you very, very much. I went to the
hospital in Kuopio to see the Father Superior. They are
giving him radiation. I went by boat, in second class, and
sat in the dining-room. It was interesting to observe how

people live, and I recalled the words of John the Theologian: 'For all that is in the world, the lust of the flesh and the lust of the eyes and the pride of life' [I John 2:16] and this saying proves true at every step. Everywhere one sees only vanity and pride, and in this maelstrom the whole stormy world whirls round with its deceitful fascination. St Isaac the Syrian said: 'The world is a flatterer and a deceiver and will understand its own state only when it passes into eternity'. By the grace of God I am well. I did receive all your letters, you can rest assured, and I remember the content of each letter, but I confess that I do not keep them.

Warm thanks to you again, my spiritual child, for all your deeds and good wishes. Write, and I will answer as far as I am able.

22   *16 September 1947*

Christ is in our midst!

By the grace of God I am well. The grain has been harvested from the fields and threshed. I did fall ill during the threshing; I caught a cold – dust, sweat and draught. Now they have begun to dig potatoes: there are many potatoes and with good weather it will be done in two weeks. When one is healthy it is good to work, it is even instructive, sometimes to the point of tears. Each works according to his strength. Conversations are varied, of course; sometimes arguments take place, even abuse: we are human beings and inevitably what is human comes into it.

The priest-monk Michei died peacefully on Monday the fifteenth at three in the morning and was buried on Wednesday. Remember him, Lord, in thy Kingdom. And your turn, my spiritual child, and mine will come inevitably. Lord, help us sinners to make a good beginning and save us sinners by the dispensations which Thou knowest. Amen.

23   *27 October 1947*

Do not be too shut off from others. If you go to name-day parties, go, but be concentrated there too, in the presence of God. You have no one there with whom it would be suitable to share your experiences openly, which might be useful, and you must not speak with inexperienced people, for they can distort things. St Peter Damascene said: 'In the beginning I suffered a great deal at the hands of inexperienced advisers'.

Do not be surprised if people sometimes look at you as though you were queer when you speak to them, because their understanding is different from yours. Be discriminating and speak in accordance with their turn of mind.

It is bad that you are not able to be silent. St Arsenius the Great always repented of much speaking, but never of silence. After reading the books of the Holy Fathers, of course you find Bishop Theophan's books dry. They can be compared this way: the Holy Fathers' writings are

27

cream, and Bishop Theophan's are skimmed milk with water added.

You write that remembrance of death is a great virtue. St Chrysostom prayed to be given remembrance of death. Remembrance of death is a gift of God. Somewhere it says: 'Remember your end and you will sin no more'.

The Lord keep you, my spiritual child.

24   *29 October 1947*

... Go on praying as you are praying now. The Jesus Prayer and remembrance of God, that He sees all and knows all – these are identical with prayer. Do not strive for higher things, such as tender feeling and tears – these come unexpectedly, of course, by the grace of God. And it is good that you have the urge to pray in your busy life of office work and household cares. Do not be surprised that you could not open your mouth to speak with your acquaintance. I too have experienced the same thing. It even occurs in the Holy Fathers. Read what St Cassian says about it on page 187 in chapter 23,[10] starting at the tenth line from the top. The Lord give you wisdom.

All goes well at the monastery for the time being. We live the ordinary monastic life, and as to what lies ahead for us, may the Lord's will be in everything. I refer to the present, outward, earthly life, but what is important is the hour of death which awaits each one of us inescapably. This temporal life of ours is the path to eternity and the

10. In the First Conference of Abbot Moses.

preparation for it. Lord, help us sinners to do what is pleasing in thy sight, and grant us a Christian ending to our lives.

25   *5 December 1947*

I received your cordial note. I was happy with your last words: 'I am not troubled at all, but peaceful'. According to the Holy Fathers, that is how it should be: if you falter in some virtue, you must not tremble; if you fall – get up; if you fall again, get up again; and so on till the final hour of death. O Lord, glory to thy mercy. Great is thy goodness, that Thou hast given repentance to us sinners, for Thou didst come to earth not for the righteous, but for us sinners.

You did draw up pure water, but a toad had unexpectedly got into the well. Throw it away and the life-giving water will still be pure. I am glad that you have begun to get at the root of the meaning of the spiritual life. It is a great blessing that the Holy Fathers have left us advice based on their own experience. Look at the books more often.

The Lord keep you; be saved.

26   *20 December 1947*

There was no reason for you to be troubled about your dispirited letter. We are human beings and our states of mind are changeable. It is good that you write your experiences; they do not disturb me. On the contrary, I am pleased when you write straight from the shoulder; do write what you experience.

Imagination and memory are one inner sense. Sometimes the memory of former events hits us on the head like a hammer. At such a time concentrated prayer is needed, and patience too. Our memory must be filled by reading the Holy Gospel and the writings of the Holy Fathers; in other words, the mind should not be idle. Former events must be replaced by other thoughts, and gradually the former recollections will be crowded out and the melancholy will pass. In one heart two masters cannot live together.

Sinful passions can never be satisfied; the more you feed them, the more food they demand. They are like a dog which is used to licking the butcher's block. As soon as you take a stick and drive him away, he will no longer come to the block. The holy Apostle says: 'Look carefully how you walk' [Eph. 5:5], and also 'forget what lies behind and strain forward to what lies ahead' [Phil. 3:13].

A woman I know sent me a long letter in which she writes that the Jesus Prayer has begun to be established in her. What a joy that there are people praying in the world. She was in Germany. Now she has gone to South America. Good journey! Help her, Lord! Now, my spiritual child, let us, you and me, follow this woman's example and take up this short prayer more vigorously. Help us, Lord. You are now accustomed to your work and do not need to think about it. Fill your memory with prayer and thoughts of God. The time is ripe, begin! Without prayer, life is full of sighs: but prayer when it becomes a habit rejoices the heart and gives it peace, which is a blessed state. At times even here on earth those who pray get a foretaste of future bliss.

27   *1947*

. . . The Lord in his mercy let you have a small taste 'that the Lord is good'. You have now begun to understand a little the meaning of 'the Kingdom of Heaven is within you'. At such a moment the visible world no longer seems to exist. Now you understand the state of bliss and what are the causes of its leaving us. The Lord make you wise! Your way of fighting with passions is right, because passions have no order. Whichever passion strikes, fight against it. However, realize that you cannot overcome them by your own powers; in this if nothing else you have to call on the Lord for help. But condemnation is a great evil. Those who condemn usurp God's prerogative, and the Lord lets such people fall into the same sins. The cause of condemnation is inattentive living. Take a good look into your own heart to see how much is there that is rotten.

Your health is not enviable either. But do not be dejected – yield to God's will. We all shall die, tomorrow if not today.

Here is something I have noticed; it is a great mistake and a weakness to be overanxious to prolong our life. Anyway life and death are in God's hands, and the Lord said, 'Seek first the Kingdom of God and his righteousness, and all these things shall be yours as well'. And so our concern and striving should be to live according to his commandments, and to free our hearts from passion.

I wrote to you not to get excited. I meant that you should not strive for higher things prematurely – everything comes in its own time. If we prepare room in our hearts by fulfilling God's commandments, then that good state will come, but it will come to us unexpectedly. Our task is to strive and work, but everything else depends on grace. One further remark; if you condemn, tears and tenderness will not come to you. The Lord give you understanding and keep you!

28   *30 December 1947*

Christ is in our midst!

In your last letter you told of having the same experiences again. But now, thank the Lord, they are over. If there were no sorrows, neither would there be salvation, said the Holy Fathers. Sorrows have two uses: the first is zeal towards God and whole-hearted thankfulness. The second is being delivered from vain cares and concerns. It is clear from the writings of the Holy Fathers that they too, like us, became depressed and faint-hearted, and they even went through experiences that they did not want to commit to writing lest they should disturb those of us who were inexperienced in the spiritual life and bring us to despair. Of course, the Lord permits sorrows in accordance with our powers, in the amount that each can bear. These trials humble us. We have a kind of self-confidence, we want to succeed in the spiritual life by our own powers, and it is in such sorrows that we learn humility, that our efforts cannot achieve their aims without God's help. Ours should be the effort towards virtue, but success even in virtue depends on grace, and grace is given by God and only to the humble. No one becomes humble without humbling events.

The wise spiritual life was explained with precision by the Holy Fathers in their writings, but what they wrote can best be understood by being lived. If you yourself work to free your heart of passions, then everything will be clearer and more understandable. Holy Fathers, pray to God for us sinners, and open our small minds to comprehend your writings.

You write that your duties distract you from prayer. As you work, keep the memory of God; this too is prayer. It is good that you have this striving for the spiritual life and for prayer. This is already half of salvation, and God will help you to go further. Only do not be depressed and faint-hearted; may the Lord help you.

You also write that you have not even reached a beginning. This feeling is a good thing; it leads to humility. According to the law of spiritual knowledge, spiritual life has to be like this. The closer a man comes to God, the more he sees his faults and his sinfulness. Lord, deliver man from seeing himself as righteous. May the Lord help you and save you from eternal suffering.

I received your note and am answering it, but take my advice not as an order or law, but simply as advice. You need not accept it if you feel that it is inconsistent with Holy Scriptures and with the message of the Holy Fathers.

Do not get excited, do not strive for the highest things prematurely. In the spiritual life one does not make leaps and bounds; it has to be gradual, with patience. You have already begun partially to notice what is not good for you: worldly books, politics and unnecessary going among people. Yes, all this is harmful for a watchful person. Your way of fighting with passions is right. Work against whatever passions you notice in yourself, but not only with your own powers, but with God's help. However, pay most attention to the chief passion, the one that is troubling you most. Remember too that the work must be ours, but success depends upon grace, and grace will be given not for work, but for humility, to each in the measure of his humility. And this ability to persevere in virtue is dependent not on us, but on grace.

You should also know that a person cannot always be in one state; changes come like the weather. It is good to be on Tabor, but sometimes one has to be at Golgotha. A watchful and sober-minded person will find many opportunities to understand this. How well St Isaac the Syrian speaks of this in his 46th [72nd] chapter.

You write: 'There is little hope that I will get to where you go'. Take back those words. We have no knowledge of God's judgement and of where anyone will go. It is good that you made peace with N. Always act in that way, even though there is no cause for enmity on your part. The Optina[11] startsi are spirit-bearing. They are steeped in the spirit of the Holy Fathers. I respect them highly and revere them. In conclusion I would like to say: 'Bear one another's burdens, and so fulfil the law of Christ' [Gal. 6:2]. What you do not want done to you, do not do to others; that is the golden rule. Remind yourself often of the hour of death and never condemn anyone for anything, because whatever you condemn others for, you will fall into the same sins; it is never otherwise.

I call God's blessing upon you.

30   *5 January 1948*

. . . The Lord knows our weakness and He has granted us daily repentance until we die. St John of the Ladder writes: 'Previous habit often tyrannizes even over him who deplores it. And no wonder! The account of the judgements of God and our falls is shrouded in darkness, and it is impossible for us to comprehend it' [5,29]. He says further: 'Do not be surprised that you fall every day; do not give up, but stand your ground courageously. And assuredly the angel who guards you will honour your patience' [5,30]. St Abba Dorotheos says: 'A man who drinks once is not called a drunkard, nor is a person who once commits fornication called a fornicator . . . but only when these are habits' [p. 179]. According to spiritual knowledge, even punishments

11. Hermitage in the diocese of Kaluga, south of Moscow.

differ. Lenience should be shown towards a person who strives for virtue and falls, for he was not aiming at sin, but was unexpectedly tempted. But severe punishment is needed for one who does not strive for virtue so that he may come to his senses and do so. Thus your single weakness too deserves lenience; a mere trifle. More likely a touch of pride is disturbing you. 'How could I let this happen?' The Lord keep you.

31   *13 January 1948*

. . . You are being asked to help in the church. God bless you; work hard. In olden times such workers were called deaconesses. Of course they had many other duties too, but this is enough for you. Do not be troubled about not being able to listen to the service. St Makarios writes: 'Work is done for those who pray, and prayer is done for those who work'. You see, you get a general wholeness. I have written this in my own words form memory – if you have Makarios' writings, read the third chapter.

It is good that you are making an effort to advance in prayer. Prayer is more precious than anything else, but it is more abhorrent to the enemy than anything else. He puts many obstacles in our way, but there is no need to fear him. The Lord gives prayer to him who prays. God bless you; work; pray.

Christ is in our midst!

I congratulate you on receiving Christ's Holy Mysteries. Your confession with Father N was upsetting, but what can be done? Be patient, do not be dejected. The white clergy[12] somehow always require severe feats on the part of monastics. Actually a monk differs from a layman only in being unmarried, and otherwise laymen too should and must live the same kind of life, i.e. according to the commandments. The Lord's commandments are common to all. The monks withdrew from the world simply in order to have a better chance to fulfil the Lord's commandments. At that time, of course, the monastic life was flowing in a different channel, because of the world situation. Those who have zeal for the spiritual life must adapt themselves to this life outwardly, but the most important thing is to put all their effort into inner work. The holy Apostle Paul says: 'While bodily training is of some value, godliness is of value in every way' [1 Tim. 4:8].

In the Holy Fathers I have found three prophecies about the last monks, and Bishop Ignatii Brianchaninov thinks that we are already the last monks. 'The last monks will not have monastic occupations; temptations and misfortunes will overtake them, and those monks who endure them will be higher than us and our fathers'. Of course, the world cannot know this, for it knows and loves only outward show.

12. Parochial, married clergy.

You ask how you should fast. There is a great deal to be said about fasting. I will write briefly. We should be obedient to the Church and fulfil exactly what it commands. If something is left undone through human weakness, we should reproach ourselves and repent. St Diadochos writes: 'Fasting has value as a means to chastity for those desiring it, but fasting in itself is nothing to God' [ch. 47.7]. In the first week of the Great Fast, on Monday evening the Holy Church sings: 'A true fast is alienation from evil, restraint of the tongue, refraining from wrath, putting aside of lusts, accusations, falsehood and perjury. Weakening of these is a true and acceptable fast.'

A learned man and very great ascetic, St John Cassian, writes: 'For if we fast because we think it is sinful to take food we shall not only gain no advantage by our abstinence but, according to the Apostle, shall actually contract grievous guilt for impiety, because we shall be abstaining from foods which God has created to be received with thanksgiving by the faithful and those who know the truth. For everything created by God is good and nothing is to be rejected if it is received with thanksgiving [1 Tim. 4:3]; for if a man thinks that a thing is profane, to him it is profane [Rom. 14:14]. And therefore no one was condemned simply for taking food, but only when something was joined with it or followed afterwards, for which he deserved condemnation.'[13]

As for the rich people who do not want to pay you the money they owe, think it out yourself and with God's help

13. The First Conference of Abbot Theonas, ch. 13.

decide on the basis of Holy Scripture. The Lord give you wisdom. It is needless for you to be troubled and think you have left some sin unconfessed. The only deadly sins are those of which you are aware and do not repent.

Again you write about dreams, that you have read in the Holy Fathers: 'If a dream is repeated, it is a true dream'. It is not good to trust dreams. St Barsanuphius the Great writes: 'He who appears falsely once can do it even three or more times' (Answer No. 415). I am sending you some excerpts on dreams. As to the cross which you dreamed about, you should not be afraid or expect any trouble. Believe that nothing can happen to us against the will of God. You are always frightened and expecting something unpleasant to happen. This fear of yours is a physical one; it is your cross, and may the Lord help you to bear it patiently. It is good that you stopped condemning N. The Lord help her, for life is slippery at her age.

It is good that you are reading the akathists and saying the prayer six hundred times, as long as you do it attentively and do not scatter it to the winds.

Try with God's help to eradicate this dislike which you feel towards N and her parents.

Best wishes for the bright forty days' fast. The Lord help you to spend it in Christian piety.

33 *14 April 1948*

Peace be with you, and God's blessing.

Do not be depressed, be vigilant, pray to God and ask

for his help. Even if you sometimes speak a bit roughly to
N, never mind, do not lose heart. You are not an angel,
you know; it is characteristic of man to get angry. Nevertheless, try to bear her weaknesses, and the Lord will bear
yours. Do not be upset if carnal thoughts sometimes attack
you; it is natural. Only the grace of the Lord can free us
from them; yet I know that they will come back to mind
until our dying day, and not even old age is free from them.

Yes, the spiritual life is complicated. It requires deep
humility and cannot be understood by reason; it is grasped
only by experience, when one tries to live in accordance
with the counsels of the Holy Fathers. If someone asks your
advice, answer what you know, but pray inwardly before-
hand and put yourself under God's will. Speak simply, do
not philosophize, do not try to influence the person. If what
you say is useful, it is by the grace of God. N is spiritually
a babe and needs to be fed with milk. Listen patiently to
all she says: when she has expressed everything it will be
a relief to her. Tell her not to pay attention to others and
not to observe their shortcomings, for every person will
have to answer for himself before God. Let them work out
their own affairs. There is no commandment that we should
require others to love and to live a correct life. Let those
who have been appointed for the purpose by God's Providence look after others.

34   *30 May 1948*

Your interesting letter, written with feeling, arrived in good
time and I read it with love. Thanks be to our Lord Jesus

Christ that in his mercy He has freed you from the heaviness of your inner confusion. This help was according to your faith and not from me a sinner, all tangled in sins. It is good that you ran to God for help at your moments of sorrow, because our soul is created in the image and likeness of God and therefore it is only in God that we can receive help and comfort at such moments.

Know that we cannot go through life without sorrows. The Lord said: 'In the world you have tribulation' [John 16:33]. If there had been no tribulation, there would have been no salvation, say the Holy Fathers. The Lord chose the holy prophets and apostles to preach, but he did not free them from difficulties, and our Lord Jesus Christ, perfect God and perfect man (without sin) lived a sorrowful life on earth. At the hands of man, whom He created, He suffered reproach, abuse, scorn, ridicule, blows, even shameful death by crucifixion. I advise you not to be dejected. Endure, pray and try to be 'wise as a serpent and guileless as a dove' [Matt. 10:16]. If you turn to God, He in his mercy will give you wisdom and the meekness of a dove.

Here is my advice to your husband: let him make a firmer decision in his heart not to drink any more and let him pray to God for help, for the Lord hears every man; let him have no doubt about this. Our efforts alone without God's help are weak. Alcohol always flatters and cheats: you start drinking for joy, and the result is sickness of soul, languor and physical illness; I know this from experience. The Lord help him to get free from alcohol. Let him stop drinking and he will feel good, a thousand times as good.

I advise you not to contemplate monastic life. The Lord will lead you to eternal life through married life in the world. Learn to live for Christ in your family life. The Lord sees your good intention and will save you in your family life – have no doubt of this. St Makarios the Great gives the example of two women who were pleasing to God and reached perfection in the spiritual life and were even higher than the recluses. They wanted to spend their lives in monasteries, but for some reasons they had husbands. The Lord, seeing their will to serve God in a monastery, helped them to be saved while living a family life. At the present time life in monasteries is not as you picture it, and with your inexperience of spiritual life you might only be led astray by monastic life.

A few days ago I went on foot to the convent fourteen kilometres from us. I stayed there overnight, observed their life and ways, the enormous amount of work, the scanty food. The Lord help them, they have already become hardened to that life, but newcomers to the convent could hardly endure it.

Our brotherhood is getting smaller; perhaps death is already standing behind the writer of these lines and will soon cut down my life. Lord, have mercy on me, a sinner, and by the ways which thou knowest deliver me from eternal torment. Amen!

35   *3 January 1949*

Lord, give the blessing!

I read your letter, understood it all, felt it deeply, and

– I won't conceal the fact – wept. Thanks be to God that you have got through this difficult time. Do not worry about how to rearrange your life in a new way. Put yourself under God's will and pray. Time will gradually reshape things. It is good that you did not arrange a funeral meal; you had enough to do without that. Of course it was hard for you to see and experience the death of your dear mother, and you had never before been present at anyone's death. However, deaths differ. Igumen Mavrikii of Valamo struggled with death for forty days, and the priest-monk Irenei for sixty days, while yesterday we buried a 74-year-old monk who died suddenly. Before dinner he was working; after dinner he stayed in his cell alone. When they came to his cell, he was lying by the table, having given his soul to God.

Man does not die, but moves into another, eternal life. The body is of earth and goes into the earth, but the soul is of God and goes to God. That is his holy will: to appoint each person to eternal life according to his deeds. Lord, let thy mercy be upon us, for our hope is in Thee.

Do not take on too much reading, and try to be meticulous in your work. If time permits, read a chapter of a Gospel, Epistle and a reading from the Psalter, or even one Glory[14] from it. Holy Scripture is more important than the canons.

The Lord keep you.

14. Each reading from the Psalter is divided into 'Glories', so called because the word 'Glory' is printed in the Psalter at the places where 'Glory be to the Father . . .' is to be sung.

Christ is amongst us!

I got your letter and hasten to answer. Do not despair, do not be depressed; calm yourself. 'Who has not had sin and misfortune', says the Russian proverb. The Pharisees brought to Christ a woman who had been caught in adultery, and said to Him: 'Teacher, what do you say should be done with her?' [Read John 8:3–11].

God preserve you from leaving your husband; endure and pray. The Lord in his mercy will help you to get through this trouble. Your husband has humbled himself very much, he is weeping and asking forgiveness. Forgive him as God has commanded, never reproach him, and do not remind him of this temptation. It was shame and disgrace enough for him when you caught him red-handed; this is very hard for him to bear, the Lord help him. Do not make him sad, but try to look cheerful, and in that way you will relieve his soul's torment. The holy Apostle says, 'Bear one anothers' burdens, and so fulfil the law of Christ' [Gal. 6:2]. If you act in this way, your prayer will be purer. The Holy Fathers write: 'Cover your neighbour's sins, and the Lord will cover yours'. Of course this happened when he was drunk, as it did with righteous Lot, who sinned with his daughters while drunk. Read in the Bible the 19th chapter of Genesis, verses 30–38.

As soon as I had read your letter I wrote this one. Forgive its brevity. This earthly life of ours is truly a sea of ups and downs, and our little boat has to go through various misfortunes, with danger of shipwreck. Neverthless, we must not be depressed. With God's help let us try to sail across this sea and reach the quiet shelter of the Kingdom of Heaven.

In sympathy and with you in prayer.

37   *24 January 1949*

I rejoice that you are striving for the one thing needful; try not to quench the spirit. Married life should not trouble you, for it is blessed by God. Nevertheless, try to bear each other's burdens and to fulfil the law of Christ. The Lord give you wisdom!

Of course the world makes its own demands: work, bustle and care, it cannot be otherwise. If with all this you keep God in mind – that is enough. The Holy Fathers consider prayer and remembering God as the same thing. If you ever find time it would be good to do a little reading of the Gospels and the apostle's letters and to meditate on this temporal vale of tears and on death and the eternal life to come. Lord, have mercy! It is terrifying even to think that there is no end! Even though it is sometimes very hard here, and all of us poor souls groan under the weight of various troubles, still they do change; whereas there, there will be no changes at all.

You write: 'I am afraid of my unworthiness and many backslidings.' Do not forget that the Lord Jesus Christ took on our flesh and was a perfect man – without sin – not for the righteous, but for sinners. Glory to thy mercy, O Lord! The Lord knows our weakness and has granted us the healing of repentence. According to the law of spiritual knowledge, the more a man succeeds in the spiritual life, the more sinful he sees himself to be. St Peter Damascene writes: 'If a man sees his sins as sands of the sea, this is a sign of a healthy soul'. With these feelings there is no room for despair; one's soul is filled with tenderness and love towards all that live on earth. Blessed are such people, those who reach that state. It is God's reward for deepest humility and is called dispassion.

38   *5 March 1949*

Christ is in our midst!

It is good sometimes to remember one's past sins, for this gives birth to humility; but when memory of former sins leads to despair, it is clear that the enemy is trying to trouble the soul. Do not listen to him, calm yourself, do not be crushed, do not be depressed, try to drive off such disturbing thoughts by prayer. The Holy Spirit says through the prophet Ezekiel: 'If a wicked man turns away from his sins, his sins will not be remembered' [Ezek. 3:18]. The Lord does not desire the death of a sinner. So live for your family, be wise as a serpent and gentle as a dove, and do not speak of your inner life, for they will not understand you. If your husband stumbles, be patient and do not be upset, but pray more zealously; remember that you too have stumbled.

I always remember you in my prayers, and I beg you

not to forget me. The Lord in his mercy help you and your affairs.

39   *30 March 1949*

You write that spiritually you are not getting on well, 'something is lacking, probably faith and love for the Lord'. The enemy of mankind is confusing you, child. Do not listen to him. You have faith and love for God and your fear is wrong, because it is from conceit. Live as you are living, and do not ponder too much. After all, you obviously do watch yourself and want to improve, and this desire is half of salvation. What more do you need?

You have been reading the books of the Holy Fathers and cannot understand them, and now you are confused. There is such a thing as reason; you should use it and adapt yourself to the conditions of life. There are three grades in the spiritual life: beginners, intermediates and the perfect. Realize that you are a beginner, yet you are trying to slip into the intermediates and the perfect. Be content, try to keep God in mind and the Lord will help you.

40   *3 April 1949*

Christ is in our midst!

You are not the only one who has moments of faint-heartedness. All people experience these heavy times; sometimes one wants to scream.

About men's fate beyond the grave we cannot say. It is God's will. However, I have no doubt about the salvation of the soul of an Orthodox believer, but bliss is, of course, relative to the deserts of each person. As the holy Apostle said: 'Glories differ; there is one glory of the sun, and another glory of the moon, and another glory of the stars' [1 Cor. 15:41].

If a sinful soul falls into hell, the Holy Church prays for that soul and the Lord frees it from the chains of hell. I, a sinner, believe in the prayers of the Church.

By God's mercy I am well. The Lord keep you!

41   *3 August 1949*

Christ is amongst us!

. . . You want quiet in order to devote yourself to reading. Live life as it is, and adapt yourself to it as it goes on there at present. Do not be surprised that N cannot grasp John of the Ladder: he is living the outward life and has no understanding of the inner life – that is why he expressed himself about the Ladder in that way.

At the time of the oblation one can remember a Lutheran, too, among the living in the hope that the grace of God will lead him to Orthodoxy. But among the dead one should not, for he has died in hostility to Orthodoxy. But we cannot judge about the after life; God's judgements are incomprehensible to us sinners.

I received your letter and the hundred marks. I handed the money over to the monastery and am sending the letter to N. And you, servant of God, do not grieve too much over your god-daughter, thinking of her as already lost. The Lord Jesus Christ came down to earth from Heaven and took on our human flesh not for the righteous but for sinners. The Pharisees took the laws as their authority but did not themselves live according to the Law, and they could not understand Jesus Christ as true God but persecuted and condemned the Lord, saying He was: 'A Friend of sinners, for he eats and drinks with publicans' [Luke 7:34; 5:30]. They condemned a sinful woman and brought her to Him; but the Lord justified her [John 8:3–11].

Know that we are not wiser than Solomon, nor meeker than the prophet David, nor more fervent than the apostle Peter. Look in the Bible at the third book of Kings, 11th chapter; also the second book of Kings, 11th chapter; and the Gospel of Matthew 26:45. You see, the Lord in his mercy pardons and forgives sinners. And you, yourself a sinner, want to scold your godchild; she is having such a hard time and you want to add to her burden. The Holy Fathers deal very charitably with sinners. They say, 'If you see sinners, cover them with your garment, go and do not condemn them'.

Many examples and much advice could be cited from Holy Scripture and the Fathers, but I think even this that I have written is enough. Remember your own youth, how difficult it was to refrain from natural sins of that sort. And now the old lady has even forgotten the years of her youth and severely condemns young people. Pray for her, be as affectionate as you can with her; in doing that you will not sin. I am sending her five hundred marks; be so good as to give it to her. I pray God's blessing on you, with love in Christ.

43   *13 August 1949*

By the grace of God I am well, but you have begun to have headaches. What can one do but submit to God's will; none of our ailments come upon us without God's will.

See how faint-hearted your N turned out to be, and a military man at that; the military are supposed to be more manly! But so it is, that without faith in God there can be no manliness, for man is created in the image and likeness of God. Even though there are brave atheists, theirs is not normal manliness; it is sick, born of despair, pride and vanity. Bring them to their senses, Lord.

Be well, and in God's protection. Do not be dejected even if you are distracted in prayer; keep on forcing yourself to it.

44   *18 September 1949*

. . . About the seething in your heart, look into the cause carefully. You call yourself bad, and good for nothing.

Probably it is so; but, examine yourself: what do you feel when someone repeats your words?

You experienced fear after the death of N. It was because of her dislike for you. The Holy Church believes that for three days the souls of the dead visit all the places where they have lived, and when she came to you, you experienced fear. You are afraid of what kind of end will overtake you. Of course it is rather dreadful to die. Fear of death is characteristic of all people, writes John of the Ladder (chapter 6 'On remembrance of death', article 3). But despair and depression are from the enemy. Do not listen to his suggestions. Read at the end of the 126th chapter of the *Paterikon* the sayings of the startsi whose names have not come down to us.

Orthodox theologians have firmly stated that spiritualism is a 'demonic phenomenon'. The holy Apostle Paul said, 'Even Satan disguises himself as an angel of light' [2 Cor. 11:14].

45   *2 February 1950*

'O zealous Protectress, Mother of the Lord most high.'[15]

Good health to you, most God-loving handmaiden of God!

You have not yet learnt to wage war with the enemy of the human race. He came to you with his sly intrigues and you are nearly falling into despair. Calm yourself and do

15. Words from a troparion.

not be upset. It is the enemy bringing you recollections of former errors. You should not accept them; simply pay no attention. Here is what St Mark the Ascetic writes: 'When past sins are remembered in detail they harm a hopeful person. For if they bring with them grief, they repel hope; and if they are visualized without grief, they again introduce the old defilment within.'[16] And St Abba Dorotheos said: 'We should not be disturbed even when passion troubles us; for to be upset about it as a matter of foolishness and pride' [p. 194].

Fear pride above all, for it was because of pride that the first angel of light became Satan and for him the Lord has prepared eternal torment. When the enemy introduces thoughts of self-praise, that is the only time when we should recall our former sins, in order to humble ourselves. As it says in the *Paterikon*, a certain ascetic, when the enemy began to fight him with thoughts of self-praise, would say to himself: 'Old man! Look at your lechery'. As to your former frailties, my child, God forgives you, be at peace.

You have begun to have spells of ill health. What should you do? Rest in God's will: illnesses remind us of our passage into eternity. I wish you health of body and salvation for your soul. The Lord keep you.

46   *22 February 1950*

The fast has begun! Our whole good brotherhood will have Communion on Saturday. The service will be done properly

16. *Early Fathers from the Philokalia*, p. 91.

with choirs on both sides. The first two days we will have dry food: bread, potato and a cucumber each; on Wednesday a dinner of pea soup and potato, of course without butter; there will be no supper during the whole first week. My health, thank God, is good, and all the old men keep vigil and stand throughout the whole of the long services; this week they do not work.

God in his mercy help you to keep this edifying fast in Christian piety.

47   *15 May 1950*

A letter[17] to the wife of a man of another faith.

Christ is Risen indeed!

I received your letter on the 13th of May, read it and wept for joy. It is a mercy of God that you have become peaceful, and the Lord has granted you to take part in the Mysteries of Christ. I wrote that letter not with reason but with feeling, for I felt what inner anxiety you were experiencing.

My answer to the questions of your second letter is: try to be faithful to your husband, do not be false to him, and obey him in everything, excepting of course what Orthodoxy requires. It is not necessary to discuss religious topics, but if he himself raises the subject, answer what you know, but first pray inwardly to God. Teach him not by word but

17. Letters 47, 49 and 68 are addressed to the same person.

by a virtuous Christian life. Do not force him to go to church. If he himself wants to go, that is another matter; be satisfied and thankful that you are not prevented from going. Pray for him simply, like a child: 'Lord, save and have mercy on my husband N, preserve and teach him'. And leave all the rest to God's mercy and be at peace. The Lord give you wisdom.

Always be kind and polite to his mother, and when she says something unpleasant, be patient. Do not talk about religious matters with her, or you will lose your inner peace. When you are angry, do not make any decisions, and stop talking. Under the influence of anger you always sin and you say wrong things and will regret it afterwards. I picture you very clearly as you were at Valamo when you were a fifteen-year-old girl. It would be interesting to see how you look now, what you have become, but unfortunately I cannot see you. I would like to see a photograph of you and your husband. If it is possible, do send one; it would be a pleasure to see it while I am still alive.

How convenient it is now to communicate by letter, the distance is so great, and it flies so quickly. My warmest thanks to your husband for the medicine. It has not come yet, but I hope to get it soon. Give him my hearty greetings with the wish that God may give him good health and all success in his affairs. What language do you speak there and does he know Russian?

I ask God's blessing on you, my spiritual child, with love in Christ, remembering and praying for you.

I also remember your husband and his mother in my prayers. The Lord keep you.

54

You said that St Gregory of Nyssa wrote: 'All fallen beings, even the demons, will attain rebirth and restoration and will be saved.'[18] He expressed this as a conjecture and not as a firm belief. The Holy Church did not accept this opinion; all of St Gregory's writing, apart from this conjecture, is pure and orthodox. St Barsanuphius said to his pupils: 'Do not think that people, even saints can comprehend perfectly all the depths of God'. The holy Apostle says: 'Our knowledge is imperfect and our prophecy is imperfect' [1 Cor. 13:9]. And again: 'O depth of the riches and wisdom of God! How unsearchable are his judgements!' [Rom. 11:33].

Holy Scripture says that there will be eternal life and eternal suffering and we must believe firmly and not go into fine points of theology with our limited little minds and our hearts uncleansed of passions. St John of the Ladder writes: 'When our soul leaves this world we shall not be blamed, brothers, for not having worked miracles, or for not having been theologians or having attained visions. But we shall certainly have to give an acount to God of why we have not unceasingly wept over our sins' (Ch. 7:70). And St Isaac the Syrian says: 'Flee from reasonings about the dogmas as from a stampeding lion' (9th chapter). I could write much more still on this subject, but I think this is enough.

18. See *Of the Soul and the Resurrection*, p. 444; *The Great Catechism* ch. 26, p. 495f.

You delighted me with your last letter. You write that you will die a Christian, and I hope and pray that you will. Pray for your husband, but do not pester him and do not tell him to be Orthodox. By your advice you can offend him and push him away from Othodoxy. Pray and put yourself under God's will and leave all the rest to God's mercy. How was his examination?

You cannot remember my face from when you were at Valamo, but I remember yours very well, and even the conversation and the walks on the island. Believe that there is a God and a future eternal life that has no end, and that the human soul is immortal – it does not even grow old. Here I am, seventy-seven years old, and I feel young. Every old man and woman says the same; the soul animates the body; the body is of the earth and will go into the earth, but the soul is from God and will go to God. But as you live in the bustle of the world, it is naturally more difficult to accept such thoughts. Nevertheless, try to believe the whole of Scripture.

As regards singing in church, consider it yourself, pray and act on the promptings of your heart. You write that you have festive church services. That is good – it somehow lifts the spirit. We too for the present are having festive services; at feasts there are fifteen celebrants, wearing fine vestments. The Finns are very much interested in our services.

Your husband came out well in the photograph. He has a kindly soul; for the face is a mirror of the soul. But you did not come out too well, because you bit your lips for some reason, and what you had perched on your head I could not make out, even with a magnifying glass. You need not send me medicine for the heart pain; I am not as sick as you think. In the summer I worked out of doors and now I celebrate and stand through the daily services.

A big Russian thank you for the medicine for rheumatism; many of the old men use it and are grateful.

Be so generous as to forgive me for the delay in answering your letter. Yes, now you are surrounded by quite different people; it cannot be helped, endure and adapt yourself so that there will be peace in so far as it depends on you.

The Lord keep you by his mercy.

50   *1951*

I received your letter in due time. I am fully aware of your heavy sorrow, and I feel it with you. What should you do? You see, these things do not come to us against the will of God; if there were no sorrows there would be no salvation either. In any case they are very humbling for us; they pursue all of us everywhere, but in different forms. The Lord's dispensations are impossible for us sinners to understand and no mind can determine why the Lord sends different sorrows, very heavy ones to some and light ones to others. There is only one remedy for sorrows: patience and prayer, said St Mark the Ascetic.

Our great mistake is that we hardly think about our passing into the other world. Our life in this vale of tears is after all nothing but a path to eternity and a preparation for it. Oh, eternity, thou eternity unending! Although it is painful here and life is sometimes very hard, and heavy sorrows and cruel diseases strike, still there is a comforting thought: I shall die and all this will end. But what awaits us over there?

Lord! by those dispensations which thou knowest, save us sinners. Amen!

You wrote: 'You know my grief, from which I am saved only in prayerful trust in God's mercy, submitting to his good will to arrange everything providentially for our good'. It is well expressed, it even brings tears. Just this is the only way to relieve sorrow and abolish confusion. You are reading St Barsanuphius the Great. It is a very instructive book. I have been reading it all my life and can never have my fill of it.

Holy Scripture can be understood rightly only by the pure in heart, for they comprehend the will and purpose of God in the Scripture, but for people with hearts unpurified of passions it is a stumbling-block.

It was not for me to answer your letter, but I forgot my lack of learning and wrote what was in my heart.

51   *10 January 1951*

Christ is in our midst!

Most God-loving mother. Your interesting letter came in due time. You write of your experiences. After your good state there was confusion and depression again. It cannot be otherwise in this vale of tears: even God's well-pleasing saints were not free from changes like that. Read the forty-sixth [72nd] chapter in Isaac the Syrian.

You also write that an acquaintance has fallen into a sect. It is a great pity that our Orthodox have very little knowledge of their own teaching and easily turn to various sects. For all the sects, heresies and schisms are based on pride and self-suggestion. In Orthodoxy the authorities are the Ecumenical Councils and the teaching of the Holy Fathers. The Lord said: 'Blessed are the pure in heart, for they shall see God' [Matt. 5:8]. And the Holy Fathers with God's help purified their hearts of passions. They rightly knew the will of God revealed in Holy Scripture, but those who have not purified their hearts of passions cannot rightly understand the Scripture, and such people stumble over it, turn away from the right path and go in different directions. One could say that they leave the big ship and sit down in a frail boat and want to sail across the sea of life, and they are perishing in the waves of vain sophistries. They dig out texts to justify their error.

I have not enough time to carry on a correspondence with your acquaintance. Let her read Bishop Theophan's book, *The Way to Salvation*. She will find in it solutions to her problems. May the Lord give her wisdom.

52   *20 January 1951*

You write that you have become a bustler and have little zeal to rise up from the ground. Do not be irritated; be satisfied with what you have: a striving for the one thing needful. Each person has his own form of life. Adapt yourself to your position and contrive to do everything for God's sake. Do not aspire to a contemplative life. Try to lead an active life. As I have already said to you: try to fulfil the Gospel commandments, for the judgement at the Second Coming will be according to the Gospel. Furthermore, do not see God as a severe chastiser. He is very kind. Glory to thy compassion, O Lord! If you happen to falter in virtue – do not tremble, for our nature is very changeable. Only angels are unchanging in virtue. According to the Apostle: 'Forget what lies behind and press on' [Phil. 3:13].

Nowadays I read books very little; I only reread the places I have marked in them at various times. I do not keep a definite rule of prayer; I try to keep the rule of the publican. I like best to read the Gospel, Epistles and Psalter with the commentaries. When I go to bed I try to say the Gospel from memory as far as I know it; this is very good for me. I have not found any like-minded person with whom to talk about the one thing needful. Oh what a great blessing it is for us sinners to have the writings of the Holy Fathers; when I start to read it is just as if I had never read them! Today I read the thirty-fourth [58th] chapter of St Isaac; it is splendid. Nowadays the thought of eternal life occupies me. Eternity – and there is no end; it is awe-inspiring! Here on earth, hard as life may be, – whether with intense sorrows or severe illnesses – yet these things do end with a person's death. Some say at difficult moments: if only death would come soon! It is some comfort that sufferings will end, but in the future life which awaits us eternity has no end. Lord! Forgive us sinners. It is comforting to read the Gospel. Sometimes I get up in the night and read a chapter and lie down and repeat it; the thought of God's compassion even brings tears. Amazing is God's compassion towards us sinners: He took on our flesh and became a true man (without sin); I won't hide from you the fact that I am weeping as I write these lines. I write to you not out of vanity but simply to share my experiences as with a like-minded person.

This week I am serving and I will remember you in my prayers. The Lord keep you. Please distribute the prosphoras:[19] do not omit yourself – take two.

I pray God's blessing for you, with love in Christ.

53   *3 February 1951*

You ask whether you can go to a meeting. Decide for yourself. According to, the advice of St Barsanuphius the Great, pray first; where your thought inclines – act on that. However, it is not the meeting that causes your confusion, but your conceit. Why do they speak like that and not in the way that is good for me? But do this: during the meeting pray with attentiveness, then you will be at peace and the whole conversation will be more clear to you.

Today, the third, the monk-deacon Kornely was buried. You probably remember him – he always sang the prayer services. He was ill only three days. I gave him Communion each day. In the morning I had given him Communion

19. Altar bread.

and in the night at twelve o'clock he died, so quietly that the four monks who live with him did not even hear. At twelve o'clock they looked at him, and he had already died, eyes closed and hands folded on his chest. A blessed ending.

54   *2 May 1951*

See how weak in spirit you turned out to be. They took you away from your task of obedience and your heart began to ache and you even say; 'They drove me out in an ugly way, like a little slut'. Your sorrow is nonsensical, and you haven't even got anything to take offence at. You must be satisfied and thankful that now you can stand in church without anything to bother about; you know, you wrote to me before, that you were not very content with this task of obedience. And now when they have replaced you, your heart is oppressed with grief. It is good that you became aware and repented. God forgive you. However, realize that without humiliating events we do not become humble.

We read the Holy Gospel and forget the sufferings of the Saviour. He was perfect God and perfect man (without sin); for our salvation He endured revilement, reproach, spitting, blows on the cheek, beating on the head with a stick and a shameful death on a cross; forgive us, Lord for our negligence and inattention to thy sufferings! And what goes on here among us? They did not even say a word of reproach, and your heart was grieved. This means there is no humility – but arrogance. Without humility there is no salvation and our struggles will have been in vain. The

Lord gives his gifts not for works, but for humility, so the Holy Fathers teach us. In time of sorrow one must read the Holy Gospel and the writings of the Holy Fathers.

55   *The Day of the Holy Trinity, 17 May 1951*

Letter to a novice

. . . Do not be depressed, my spiritual child, and do not despair of the salvation of your soul; those thoughts are from the evil demon; simply do not accept them. For spiritual guidance I advise you to look more often at the holy Abba Dorotheos' book. And try to live by his advice; the Lord make you wise. I have grown to old age in a monastery, but I go on studying this book. It is my handbook and I look into it nearly every day, for it is called the monastic primer.

When you work with the sisters you can talk with them but let there be no condemnation or slander. However, the Holy Fathers said: 'Spiritual conversation is silver, but silence is golden'. As for idle talk – use your own sense.

I want to tell you this too. Do not start up a special friendship with anyone; otherwise you will suffer many useless sorrows and your life will be full of sighs. Try to put your own little will behind you. Do not undertake great feats and never condemn anyone for anything. Do not take notice of other people's weaknesses, but look at your own, of which you will, of course, find plenty. The passions about which you write we cannot conquer by our own powers

63

without God's help. We should try to eradicate them, but to overcome them altogether depends on God's grace. You are still young. Do not trust yourself, but be humble until you reach the grave. Life is slippery at your age. However, if something does happen through human weakness, do not be crushed and lose heart; for we are not wiser than Solomon, nor meeker than the prophet David, nor more zealous than the apostle Peter. The Lord knows our human weakness, and He gave us repentance to help us. There is no sin that can conquer God's mercy, and all our sins, whatever they may be, are like a handful of sand thrown into the great ocean, compared with God's mercy.

Our monastery life is still glimmering a little. Many of the old men walk with the help of a stick. There are no newcomers, since at the present time young people are not educated in a religious spirit. According to a remark of Bishop Ignaty Brianchaninov, we are already the last monks. However, God's dispensations are incomprehensible to us sinners. Lord, thy will be done in everything.

I pray God's blessing on you; may the Lord and the Queen of Heaven help you in difficult moments.

56   *16 August 1951*

You complain that you cannot concentrate on prayer – you are still 'without feeling'; you acknowledge your negligence but not the influence of outward affairs. Yes, prayer is sweet, but it requires great labour and, as Abba Agathon said: 'Prayer requires struggle until one's last breath'. However, you must realize that every mode of life has its own order. You live in the world – so try to do with a good conscience the task to which you have been assigned by God's Providence. Do not condemn anyone for anything; whatever you yourself dislike, refrain from doing to others. You would not like people to say unpleasant things to you or to reproach you or annoy you or treat you roughly, or speak ill of you, so do not do anything of that sort to anyone. This is the proper order for your mode of life; do try to live this way. If your conscience has any accusation against you, repent to the Lord. What you are striving for is the mode of life proper for monastic hermits, and it requires complete freedom from cares and, above all, humility. Without humility all ascetic efforts are in vain. But you are occupied all day with cares and troubles. How can you concentrate in prayer? If you find a free minute, read the Gospel a little, and the Epistles, and have a look at the books of the Holy Fathers. The Lord give you wisdom.

As regards your conversation, judge for yourself. Nevertheless, if a person is chosen for some duty that he does not himself aspire to, it means that it is God's will and the Lord will help. But there is no place to which one can flee from annoyances; no matter where a person goes – they will go with him.

57   *22 October 1951*

. . . You moan that you have no good deeds to your credit! Have you really no good deeds – at work, are you not

65

absolutely loaded with them? If you add to that: do not condemn others, and what you do not want to be done to you do not do to others either, that is enough for you, be at peace. But to put one's nose in the air because of a good position would in my opinion be utter madness for a Christian who aspires to a spiritual life. The Lord give you wisdom.

It is unreasonable, even sinful to think that you 'would be lost' without me. Read the Bible and the Holy Fathers and be wise. What does my advice mean when I myself am groping my way? If I write something, I get it from the same sources. I am like a smoke sauna; I wash others clean, but I stay just as black.

The Lord protect you.

58   *4 January 1952*

. . . You keep condemning yourself and regarding yourself as good for nothing and the worst of all people, but these are only words with you. You feel that you are not bad. If you felt the way you say you do, you would not condemn others for anything and you would not feel insulted over my having called N more intelligent than you. Ha-ha-ha! How muddle-headed you are. You go on to write that I should pray and beg the Lord to 'make you good'. Again what a muddle-headed request! Another laugh: she will live in an off-hand way and the old man will beg and pray God that she should become good. But this is not in accord with spiritual knowledge; neither God nor I can help you if you yourself do not work at it devotedly, the Holy Fathers have said.

Yesterday a monk came to me and said: 'I have a very big sin and I do not know whether the Lord will forgive me'. I asked: 'What is it?' 'Blasphemy against God and the Holy Mysteries.' I said to him: 'In these thoughts there is no sin, for they are from the devil and are called suggestions; they are not sins. Do not pay attention to them and lift your mind to some scriptural subject'. I talked further with him on this subject and gave him John of the Ladder to read about blasphemous thoughts [23,38ff.].

Today, the 4th of January, the Holy Church celebrates the seventy Holy Apostles. Of these, five Apostles fell away: Judas, Nicholas – he was a bishop, Phygelus – he was a bishop, Hermogenes – he too was a bishop, and Demas – he was a priest and became a worshipper of idols. I used to wonder: why did the Lord choose them as apostles to preach? He knew that they would fall away. But once during a service it somehow became clear to me that the Lord in his mercy calls everyone to Himself, but He does not destroy our free will. And if someone willingly turns from virtue to a depraved life – he is himself to blame, since he did not make the effort with his free will to please God. One became fond of money, another became fond of this temporal life, and the others the same. We should use our free will to work to please God; then grace helps us. But if we do not make the effort, even God's grace will not help; our work and God's grace go together.

They say that your husband drinks. What should you do?
Do not grieve, and do not condemn him. Everyone has his
weaknesses and inadequacies, you know. He too is not
without weaknesses and not without inadequacies. So learn
from each other, bear each other's burdens and thus fulfil
the law of Christ. The Lord give you wisdom.

How fast the time flies! The Nativity of Christ, the Epi-
phany and the New Year were awaited and all of that has
gone. Now Easter is on its way. Of course, first we must
look to the Great Fast, as the way of preparation, in order
to celebrate the Bright Feast of Christ more perfectly.

Here is something I have noticed: as old age advances,
time flies faster, it feels as if everything was already at an
end. The time of passing into eternity is approaching, and
somehow even all interests have gone. But open the minds
of young people and you will see how fantasy plays in them:
they are happy, they will get good suitors, they will be rich,
their family life will go well, and a great deal more along
this line. These pictures will pass through their heads, and
again they will be alone.

Life in our monastery still glimmers gently, but our
brotherhood has grown old. It is just like an almshouse,
each one older than the next. If I live to February, I will
be seventy-nine – a respectable age, and I am already ripe
for passing on into eternity. I thank God that I have
reached such an age and that it was granted to me, a
sinner, to spend my whole life in a monastery. I have not
known the vanity of the world, filled with cunning, vain-

glory, hypocrisy, falsehood and arrogance. Can anybody in the midst of these vices ever feel peace and tenderness in his soul? I suspect not.

What do you and your husband feel when you come home after the theatre and masquerades? Of course you get some kind of impression there, and you will be looking forward to when you can go to the same places again and again, if only sickness does not interfere. That is the way the worldly life of vanities goes. But when a person is lying on his deathbed or in sickness – and that is when he is confronted with unexpected experiences such that all his past life passes before him with the events which he lived – then only will he realize that this world is a fraud.

I ask God's blessing on all your family.

60   *18 February 1952*

You have no children and you want to have them; your desire is natural in the order of things. However, everything can happen: children may be no joy to their parents, but a great sorrow. Let us give ourselves over to God's will, for He knows our needs before we ask anything. If children will be a benefit, there will be children without a surgical operation. Let us pray this way: Lord, Thou knowest our needs before we ask anything; in thy goodness, bless what will be good for us. Amen.

61   *27 April 1952*

I have been answering various people's letters, and now
your turn has come to get an answer. It is good that you
like to be at home and do not invite anyone to visit you.
Even if people talk, stick to your convictions. It is also good
that you keep a little farther away from parish affairs. But
when something concerns you and you must speak – do not
forget to pray first. You will discover from experience how
useful it is. Even though it is rather difficult to suffer
afflictions, it is very beneficial. And we should prepare
ourselves with God's help, to endure abuse, reproach, scorn
and ridicule. If we prepare ourselves, then when they come
it will be easier to bear them. People are inconstant; today
they praise you, but tomorrow they cast you off.

62   *26 June 1952*

I received your parcel and letter in good time. For the
parcel I cannot thank you but must give you a scolding.
You yourself live in want and you have taken it into your
head to send parcels, even to a strict monk who should feed
on bread and water according to the example of the Holy
Fathers. I speak severely to you so that this will not happen
again.

You write that you are 'lazy and careless' and you ask
me to berate you. How can I scold you when I myself am
old and afflicted with the same ailment, and more than
you. However, let us not be depressed and lose hope; let us

be humble and make a beginning even though we have come at the eleventh hour [Matt. 20]. But the Lord is very merciful and gives the same pay as to those who have worked since morning. Glory, Lord, to thy compassion!

The Lord gives prayer to those who pray. Realize, however, that prayer requires struggle, even to the hour of death. Be satisfied with the quality of your prayer as it is. Do not aspire to tenderness and tears, but when they come, stop and wait until they pass of their own accord. Prayer and memory of God are equivalents; one can walk or be doing something, and think of God – and this is also prayer.

Try not to condemn anyone, nor to have hostility towards anyone; otherwise your prayer will come to nothing. The Lord give you wisdom.

63   *17 September 1952*

I am happy that you have begun to read spiritual books. You will experience for yourself the spiritual benefits of this reading. Good Luck! Keep up your interest in the spiritual life.

Tell her to pray for her husband's parents and to give their names in church for the repose of their souls. Even if her heart does not want to, she should make herself do it; otherwise God will not accept her prayer for the salvation of her own soul. The Lord commanded us even to love our enemies [Matt. 5:44 and Luke 6:27–35]. The Lord Himself even prayed for those who crucified Him: 'Father, forgive them, for they know not what they do' [Luke 23:34]. When

St Stephen the Archdeacon was stoned, he prayed: 'Lord, do not hold this sin against them' [Acts 7:60], and having said this, he died.

In the Holy Gospel the Lord many times speaks of forgiving offences. But you in your weakness, and perhaps also pride, do not want to remember your offenders. Realize that our judgement will be at the Second Coming according to the Gospel, for heaven and earth will pass away, but not an iota, not a dot will pass from the law [Matt. 5:18]. It is terrible not to fulfil the Gospel commandments: pray that the Lord may soften your heart, not to remember injuries, and that you may, be able to pray for the parents of your husband. Maybe these lines of mine will seem severe to you, but I cannot write otherwise.

St Barsanuphius the Great says: 'Mother Sarah said: "If I want to please all people, I will have to repent at their doors."'

About my illness, you need not grieve – it would be wrong of you. Whether my life in this vale of tears will be much prolonged is unknown; even though it has become rather difficult to celebrate, I receive Communion at the altar, go to the services, to the refectory and for walks out of doors.

It is not necessary to fear weakness, for the Lord came down from Heaven for the weak. If a man recognizes his weakness and repents, the Lord in his mercy will not remember his weaknesses and sins. The most necessary things to fear are devilish pride, vainglory, hostility and condemnation, but weaknesses serve to humble our imagined piety. Do not be surprised that good people who are close to the Church and are deep believers are always heaping abuse when they are wounded. These people are superficial, they have no understanding of the one thing needful, and so outward piety does them no good. But it is necessary to pray for N and have sympathy for her heavy cross.

Recently a monk said to me: I am tired of living; if only I would die! I would like to be turned into nothingness.' But I kept silent; I know that he will not accept my advice. You see, all monks are well read and each understands theology and the teaching of the Holy Fathers in his own way, rightly or wrongly, and they hold to their convictions. For such people, advice from the outside is inappropriate; they themselves are keen to teach others. Oh, how well the holy Abba Dorotheos expressed it: 'Each is careless and does not keep a single commandment, yet he holds his neighbour accountable for the commandments' [p. 144]. How many examples of this one sees in the course of a day! Of course I do not pay attention to them, for this is an ordinary phenomenon. If we observe ourselves we see utter chaos in our heart, and phenomena like this do not touch our heart.

64   *4 December 1952*

The Lord's ways are inscrutable to us sinners; no mind can understand, and let us not question to whom the Lord gives what kind of cross. If she reviles us and puts us to shame, let us not be upset and condemn her, but pray the Lord to help her and save her from misfortunes and sorrows.

Realize that slander and humiliation, unpleasant though they are, are very useful and salutary for us. If you watch yourself more closely, you will find out from experience. We must fear praise, for it nourishes vainglory and conceit. Woe to us if praise is higher than our deeds.

Poor N has started drinking again. Give them my greetings and tell them not to get depressed. The Lord help them to improve.

I ask God's blessing on you all.

65   *12 December 1952*

Christ is in our midst!

. . . You write of your illnesses that they are sent by God for your sins.

No, you must not think that way. The Lord's thoughts are unsearchable, and our limited little minds cannot understand why different kinds of sicknesses and sorrows are given by God to different ones of us sinners. But realize that in this vale of tears, this temporal life, we cannot escape them.

The Lord give you wisdom! Don't think of God as a very stern judge and punisher. He is very merciful; He took human flesh and suffered as a man, not for the saints' sake but for sinners like you and me. We must not despair, for there is no sin that exceeds God's compassion. It is always the devil that brings despair; one must not listen to him.

Try as far as possible to fulfil the Lord's commandments. Judge no one for anything and you will not be judged. If you watch yourself, you will of course find sins, which will show you that you have no cause to condemn others. And also: 'Whatever you do not wish for yourself, do not do it to others either', and other Gospel commandments.

You also write that you used to pray better, but now you do not hear the Lord knocking at your heart. Do not think like that either! Your prayer used to be dreamy and you thought something of yourself, but now you have begun to understand a little – so you can see yourself more truly. The closer a person comes to God, the more sinful he sees himself to be. St Peter Damascene writes: 'If a person sees his sins like the sands of the sea, that is a sign of a healthy soul'. This is the position of the saints, and they are experienced in the spiritual life. But people want to see themselves as correct in every respect.

Of course it would be good to have a personal talk about the spiritual life, for it is difficult to write in a letter about the subtleties of the spiritual life.

Be thankful to God that in his goodness He freed you from the hatred you felt towards your husband's parents. And in future try never to have hostility towards anyone, for life and death depend on the neighbour.

The holy Apostle Paul lists the degrees of saints, comparing some to the sun, others to the moon, and others to the stars; and there are great differences among the stars [1 Cor. 15:41]. But may you and I be tiny stars if only we can be in the same heaven. And if something does happen because of human weakness, we should not be dejected.

75

Let us be humble, know our weakness and repent. Man's characteristic is to fall, but the devil's is not to repent.

Lord, let thy mercy be upon us, as our hope is in Thee. Amen!

66   *12 December 1952*

Your warm letter came in good time. I thank you with all my soul for your good wishes and sympathy for my infirmity.

I am glad that your operation was successful. It was not my feeble prayer that helped you, but your faith in my prayers. This is clear from the Holy Gospel; many times the Saviour said: 'According to your faith be it done to you'.

I was in the hospital in the town of Joensuu for two weeks. Now, with God's help, I feel well.

I know very well the desire of a woman to have a child and her sorrow at not having children. It is my wish that the Lord may fulfil the desire of your heart. Let us be well inclined to God's will and await his mercy.

You offer your services to help me in some way. I have everything; there is no need to send my anything. But when you have received this letter, write me how you feel. I shall wait patiently for your letter.

67   *27 December 1952*

... The holy monk Moses of Scetis said: 'Of the monks who came to me for advice, some I comforted and they departed with profit to their souls; but to others, to my shame, I could say nothing useful and they departed unconsoled'. Thus even saints sometimes were unable to give comfort and say anything helpful. Who am I to be able to give comfort in sorrows? If anyone has received benefit from my advice, it was through his own faith. Priest-monk Barnabus of Holy Trinity Lavra, a clear-sighted staretz, advised a merchant on an important matter, but it did not prove right, and an awkward situation resulted. At Valamo the schema-priest-monk Alexy, whom Father Ephrem greatly respected, gave advice about something to a certain igumen, but then he changed his mind and all night he rolled around like a spindle.

To those who turn to me, small-brained as I am, I will give my opinion and then always say: 'But consider the matter yourself'. Right advice can be given only by holy people, like St Seraphim of Sarov and Serge of Radonezh. How can I give right advice when I myself am groping?

68   *17 January 1953*

As to your last letter, I find it very difficult to offer any advice. But it is a joy to hear that you have a spark and love for God burning in your soul. God grant that this spark and love for God may last until your grave. Try to sustain it.

When you arrived in New York, your husband looked for an Orthodox church and even stood through the whole Easter service; and now he has changed very much and does not even want you to take his son to church. Unfortunately, we can expect that he will not want you to go to church either. Even though he is a good man, as you write, he has already changed under the influence of his relatives. But a flaming love without religion is very insecure. I pity you for having fallen into such an environment. However, do not be depressed or discouraged. Pray and hope for help from God and the Queen of Heaven.

Do not talk with him about religion . . .

I ask God's blessing on you and your husband's mother. When you are sad, write to me.

69   *30 January 1953*

You keep writing about your troubles and your inner disorder. Realize that it cannot be otherwise in the temporal life, and do not try to find out from whom and through whom they come, for they do not come without God's permission. If not even a hair of our head will perish, how much more sure is God's protection of man. It is also said: 'By your endurance you will gain your lives' [Luke 21:18–19]. I have already written to you before that there is just one way to deal with sorrows: prayer and patience.

At a time of trouble wait for peace, and when there is peace prepare for trouble. In this temporal life peaceful and troubled phases alternate. Even the holy men of God were not free from these changes. But you want to find some new path in order to escape hard experiences. This cannot be. You haven't had abuse hurled at you or been struck on

the cheeks, have you? Just remember the patience of the
God Incarnate: the blows on the cheeks, the hitting on the
head with a stick, the spitting in his face and many kinds
of ridicule. And He endured all this for the sake of our
salvation. But we do not want, for the sake of our own
salvation, to suffer even small annoyances.

I write this and blush. I teach others, but am myself
guilty. Yet I do not lose hope; I trust in God's goodness,
that by his mercy He will save me, a negligent man.

Forgive the brevity of my letter.

With love in Christ.

70   *27 February 1953*

Letter[20] to a sick person

'O zealous protectress, Mother of the Lord Most
High . . .'

. . . You wrote that you do not deserve such favours from
me. But it may just be that in God's sight I am unworthy
of your favours to me, a sinner.

By God's mercy your serious operation went successfully.
Now you feel very miserable – what can you do? One must
endure, desiring God's will to prevail.

Let us pray like this: 'Thou, Lord, Searcher of Hearts,
already knowest our human weakness, troubles and needs
before we make our request, and we believe that not a hair

20. Letters 70, 72, 73, 75 and 78 are addressed to the same person.

will fall from our heads without thy will. Grant us to live our life according to thy will, for we sinners do not know what is good for us.'

My legs have given way, both are aching. You should see how I get up in the morning like a child that has just begun to learn to walk; then I manage to get moving and walk. It is difficult to celebrate services; I receive Communion at the altar. Nevertheless, so far I keep up my courage and go to all the services, although more and more frequently I have to sit for the service and for prayer. However, the Holy Fathers said that if you have to sit, pray attentively, the Lord receives your prayer; whereas if you pray with distraction while standing, the Lord does not hear such prayer. For attentiveness is the soul of prayer (Barsanuphius the Great 506).

Perhaps you will come to us in the summer; then let us talk about the one thing needful. But if I die, visit my grave and pray for the repose of my sinful soul.

God bless you; the Lord and the Queen of Heaven keep you.

71   *11 March 1953*

Zealous Protectress, Mother of the Lord Most High . . .

I received your letter and read it carefully. I feel that 'your spirit faints within you and your heart is desolate' [Ps. 143:4]. At the end of the letter you write: 'You probably will sense what I wanted to say'. How could I not sense it when all your feelings are mine! What you wrote, all of it, is in me as if it were copied from my heart. Now what shall we do, you and I? We cannot shout for help! Let us not lose hope; let us be patient and pray to the Lord to help us sinners to make a new beginning. You write: 'I am very stupid; I keep wanting to learn common sense, but it comes to nothing'. Well, I have lived my years in a monastery and am approaching my death, but I have not learnt common sense; I have to die a fool.

I too am by nature a lazy, weak-willed and shy person, but I do not think as you do: 'God's punishment'. It is beneficial to us; humility is born from it. We must be very fearful of pride, conceit and vainglory. Holy men were not free from similar unpleasant feelings and troubles either. Our life is like a ship on the sea – we have to endure all adversities, otherwise we cannot exist.

72   *9 August 1953*

Christ is in our midst.

I fully sympathize with your experiences. Even now you are troubled by sins committed in your youth. The enemy of mankind, the devil, made you afraid to open your distressed heart to me when you were here at the monastery.

It is always like that; when a person commits a sin, he thinks he gets consolation from it, but after he has tasted sin, the result is the opposite: great sorrow and languor of spirit, and the poor soul feels like a fish cast ashore. It is a hard situation and a person all but despairs. At such a difficult moment it would be good to talk to an experienced person, who could, of course, undoubtedly help.

There is no sin that is beyond God's mercy, and the sins of the whole world are like a handful of sand thrown into the sea.

But you write: 'Will the Lord forgive me?' You confessed and repented. The Lord forgave you and does not remember your sins. Be sure of this (Ezekiel the prophet). In your difficult time of the past your poor soul suffered and endured the cost of sin. But now be at peace and thank God for his holy mercy.

God accepts equally the Jesus Prayer and remembrance of God. Remembrance of God suits your way of life better. Prayer of the mind must proceed under the guidance of an experienced person who himself knows about it from his experience.

The Lord keep you. I ask your holy prayers.

73   *11 October 1953*

Christ is in our midst!

You like to spend time alone in the evening and have spiritual consolation. Yes, the night time helps one to concentrate. I too like that time. Complete stillness is all around, and in some special way you feel the closeness of the Lord.

You write that warmth appears when you pray. This is the way the Lord lets us sinners taste some kind of consolation so that we will not be discouraged in the work of prayer. When the warmth comes, one should stop and be with these feelings until they pass, but we should not strive for this ourselves. If you work diligently in prayer, then by God's mercy, warmth of heart will appear more often. But do not imagine that you have received something great. Try your best to keep it hidden from others. If any other things happen in prayer, write to me.

74   *1953*

The grace of God be with you, my spiritual child . . .!

I understand your confusion and confession. God forgive you, child – be at peace. After your departure the demon of vainglory also came to me and began to trouble me with various thoughts, but with God's help I repelled him right away. I thank God for his quick help and for the prayers of the holy ascetics, for I am guided by their advice in this vale of tears. What would I be without God's help? Dust of the earth and foul-smelling carrion.

How much I have said to you, spiritual child, for the good of your soul and how much spiritual advice borrowed from Scripture and the Holy Fathers I have given you, but you turn out to be very wanting in sense. You are ready even to hang a millstone round your neck and jump into the water. And do you know why? I shall explain it to you: conceit and vainglory. These do not let you see yourself as you really are. You imagine great things about yourself. This is evident from your last letter. Read the fourth chapter of part one in *Unseen Warfare*. Excuse the brevity of my letter, but I suppose I have given a satisfactory answer. If you have some doubt, write, but be candid; otherwise it will not do any good. Your questions also push me upon the path to self-knowledge. The Lord save and preserve you.

I repeat once more, God forgives you, be peaceful and calm; do not accept whisperings of the devil. The Lord give you wisdom.

75   *14 January 1954*

I received your letter. You are ill again, troubled and depressed. But do not be too depressed; your sicknesses and troubles are not chance phenomena, but sent by God, and his holy care for us sinners is past our understanding. If the Lord takes care of the birds [Luke 12:6], is it possible that he could forget you?

Your big, complicated operation has affected your whole organism; 'the earthly doctors did not help you,' as you write. I advise you now to turn to the Heavenly Doctor of our souls and bodies, the Lord. Who is your confessor there? Ask him to administer the sacrament of Unction of the Sick and give you Holy Communion. However, parish priests somehow are reluctant to anoint the sick, but ask and maybe they will agree.

As to your coming here now, it is not suitable: it is cold here, you are sick, there is the expense and loss of time.

The Lord be the protector of your soul and body. Amen.

Letter to a nun

Christ is in our midst!

I received your esteemed letter, read it with love, and rejoiced that you are zealous in prayer. God bless you – be diligent, for prayer is the main thing in the spiritual life. However, realize that the measure of its height and benefit is also the measure of its high price, i.e. great efforts. St Agathon said: 'Nothing is more difficult than to pray to God, and prayer requires a struggle to the last moment of life'. And in order that it may succeed better, try as far as you can to fulfil three conditions: have a pure conscience in relation to God, people, and things. Towards God, try to fulfil the Gospel commandments; towards people, try not to condemn or to be hostile; towards things, try to use them without attachment. These are the preparatory conditions.

Practise prayer this way: Do not represent God and the Mother of God or the saints in your mind. Contain your mind in the words of the prayer and focus your attention on the upper part of your chest, for attentiveness is the soul of prayer. You should not press attention upon the heart. If there is attention on the chest, the heart's feeling will join in. You should not aspire to tender feeling and tears, but when they come, of themselves, and warmth of heart, stop and wait until they pass. You must not think you have received something great. It comes naturally from concentration. However, it is not an illusion either.

I want to say this too, just in case, although it happens

85

seldom and to few people: tears stream down, people all look like saints, enemies do not exist, warmth invades the whole body – not warmth of the blood, but a special warmth of grace such that you cannot stand on your feet and you have to sit or lie down. This is the visit of a heavenly guest, and only a person who experiences it himself can know it; for outsiders it is incomprehensible. In prayer imitate the widow in the Gospel [Luke 18:2–9].

Sometimes you will get dryness, laziness, an influx of thoughts, sorrows, slander from people and much else, but this all will pass with God's help, if only you do not get discouraged. Do not trust yourself this side of the grave. Have humility and never condemn anyone for anything. There have been ascetics who saw the glory of the saints and had such grace from God that they performed miracles, healing the sick by laying on of hands. People glorified them and they began to form a high opinion of themselves through demonic pride. Then grace left them. They took up a dissolute life and became a laughing-stock to people. Do not be surprised that there are passions in you. They remind us that we are human beings and they humble us. Beware of conceit and demonic pride. Know too that stability in virtue depends not on us but on the grace of God, and the protection of grace is given for humility. St Isaac the Syrian says: 'If you labour at some virtue and do not see fruits and success, do not be surprised, for the Lord gives his gifts not for labour, but for humility'.

Without humility there can be no virtue. In my spiritual blindness I do not know men of prayer and cannot point them out to you. Pray yourself, for the Lord gives prayer to those who pray. If you get somewhat into the habit of prayer, then the ticking of a clock will not disturb you; but you cannot determine the time; years may go by. One young man named George mentioned in the *Philokalia*[21] had a special way of practising prayer. As for you, practise the general rules which I briefly explained to you. Do not aspire to the schema; it will not increase your spiritual progress, or are you interested in putting on a garment that has crosses on it? Strive for the one thing needful, and all the rest will be added.

In Kiev this happened: a schema–monk and a novice had been buried at the same time. When their graves were opened, the novice was wearing the habit and the schema–monk was wearing the novice's dress. There's a schema–monk for you! Poor fellow, you wore a schema and it served not for your salvation but for your condemnation. I blush as I write these lines, for I am a schema–monk too. Oh, that it may not be for my condemnation too! Yet I do not despair. The Lord is merciful; He knows our weakness and has given repentance to schema–monks too. Glory, O Lord, to thy holy mercy!

I ask your holy prayers for my need.

77   *7 February 1954*

Letter to a nun

Your long letter came and I read it with love. I am happy at the change in your life. The Holy Mother of God has in

21. Writings from the *Philokalia* on *Prayer of the Heart*, p. 145.

a marvellous way put you onto the true road that leads to the eternal dwelling places; she has even taken you under her shelter. Believe deeply that she will help you at bitter moments in your experience. In this life there is no constancy, but things change like the weather. I wrote to N about how to practise prayer: read it in the letter I wrote to her. I give you this advice not as a law or command, but simply as advice: every day repeat the 'Virgin Mother of God rejoice'[22] twelve times and the Jesus Prayer thirty-three times. Only you must try to repeat them with attention, for attentiveness is the soul of prayer. The three conditions for prayer about which I wrote to you nourish the soul in the spiritual life. It is particularly important to leave your own little will behind. Certainly this is not easy, but it is a powerful antidote to demonic pride. Pride has a way of insisting on its own way in conversation in order to keep the upper hand; it cannot bend to another's view but stubbornly persists in its own opinions.

The Holy Fathers themselves took this path and they left us these guidelines. Only on these terms can a man acquire inner peace of soul and have peace everywhere, no matter where he lives. The holy archbishop Theophilos once visited Mount Nitria and the abbot of the mount came to him. The archbishop said to him: 'With your experiential knowledge what would you say is the highest activity on the monastic path?' The staretz answered: 'Obedience and constant self-reproach'. The archbishop said: 'There is no other way than this'.

22. The Orthodox equivalent of 'Hail, Mary' [cf. Luke 1:28].

What is more, even though I can speak foolishly, I am not foolish, I have been striving to fulfil these three conditions, and by God's mercy, although I have not attained perfect peace, I am peaceful. I was made head of the Petsamo Monastery; straight from a simple monk I was ordained deacon, priest-monk and igumen. I had two weeks in which to get ready for the journey and learn how to celebrate the services. But by God's grace I was peaceful. Some monks were surprised: 'How can you get ready so peacefully; others are alarmed at moving from one cell to another, and you take this assignment so peacefully'. Many monks had a great deal to say to me. The majority advised me to refuse, saying, 'It will be a cross'. I answered, 'We do not know when and where Christ may give us a cross'. So I set out, and two other priest-monks with me. It took us sixteen days to get there, by train to Rovaniemi, and from there 500 kilometres to Petsamo, 250 with horses and 250 with reindeer. Of course it was not easy, because we did not know the language, but we got there.

We arrived in the evening and were greeted by the sound of bells; we came into the church; they invested me in a silk mantle, the royal doors were opened; I and the priest-monks who had come with me kissed the Holy Table and the shrine of St Tryphon. The brothers had all gathered in the church, the celebrants in their vestments. I had not prepared to say anything, but when I began to approach the brothers, the thought came to me: 'Say something', and I said: 'Greetings, holy fathers and brothers, I have been sent here to be your father-superior and with me are two priest-monks. We had very little time to prepare ourselves.

I have been learning to celebrate services for only two weeks, having been ordained from a simple monk. If there are mistakes in the service, please cover them with Christian love, and in practical matters I ask you to help me.' The treasurer replied, 'We will, we will help'. I continued, 'Holy fathers, the main thing is that we must try to have peace and harmony among us; if we have that, God's grace will rest upon us. Amen'. The vestry-keeper said: 'Excuse us, we cannot say anything'. The brothers all came to me for a blessing and we went to the tea that had been prepared; there was salmon pie and cheesecake. The tea was served in the abbot's cells. I stayed there overnight and then it was my permanent residence. There was plenty of space: two large rooms, two smaller ones and a bedroom. I took the monastery very simply; I lived there ten years and eight months. A deacon had been appointed abbot before me, but he went to pieces. He even began to have fits. Then I was appointed.

At Valamo I went through various obediences, all of them unpleasant for me. However, I did not get depressed, but was peaceful. Holy obedience cultivates humility and strengthens will power. The Holy Fathers even compare obedience to martyrdom. Abba Dorotheos writes very well about this. I advise you to read the book.

In general our little will is very dear to us. And suddenly we have to leave it and do the will of someone else. It is very difficult to yield to another. Only great souls are able to, but weak ones insist on their own.

And take one more rule for yourself: when you are upset, make no decisions. This is the advice of the Holy Fathers.

And another word about pride: a proud person sees only the best in himself and only the worst in others, while a humble person sees his own sins but sees good qualities in others.

78

. . . The Lord in his compassion let you have even a little taste of how good He is, as He did to the apostles on Mount Tabor. The holy apostle Peter said: 'It is well that we are here' [Mark 9:5].

But realize that sometimes one has to be at Golgotha.

Nothing arouses such opposition in the devil as prayer does. Sometimes he suggests various thoughts, even blasphemous ones, sometimes he works through people and causes various slanderings, sometimes there is dryness in the heart, laziness and much else.

I have reminded you of this so that you will not be downcast when you experience these things. You should not speak of your inner consolation or sad experiences to anyone except your confessor. People inexperienced in the spiritual life can give a wrong turn to spiritual activity.

Try not to condemn anyone for anything; you yourself know about hostility from experience. The Lord does not hear prayer where there is hatred; the whole Gospel speaks of this.

And another thing: be very fearful of imagining yourself to have received something great which others do not know. There have been ascetics who were taken up into another world and saw the glory of the saints. People praised them and they became conceited; demonic pride took possession of them, and they fell from their spiritual height into a dissolute life which made them a laughing-stock to people.

The Lord keep you and your daughter.

79 *undated*

Letter to a nun

Beloved of God:

You write that anger is getting you down and 'you have no peace and comfort'. If we do not toil and labour over our heart, there will be no peace and comfort. After all, one has to take hold of oneself and not live in an off-hand way! For the violent ravish the Kingdom of Heaven [Matt. 11:12]. Anthony the Great said to his disciple: 'I will have no mercy on you, nor will God have any, if you yourself do not make an effort. The spiritual life is like a tree: the bodily struggle is its foliage and the work of the soul is the fruit.'

Scripture says: 'Every tree that does not bear good fruit is cut down and thrown into the fire' [Matt. 3:10]. Of course bodily labour is needed, for without it there will be no fruits either. However, realize that no bodily work is a virtue; it is a means towards virtue. Many have done a great deal of work and received no fruits, for their work was external, killing the spirit: 'Do not handle, do not taste, do not touch' [Col. 2:21]. St John of the Ladder says: 'The present generation is seriously corrupt and all full of pride and hypocrisy. In bodily labours it perhaps reaches the level of our ancient Fathers, but it is not graced with their gifts, though I think nature never had such need of spiritual gifts as now. And we have got what we deserve. For God is manifested not in labours but in simplicity and humility' [26,52].

St Isaac the Syrian says: 'If you labour at any fine virtue and do not find success, or fruit, do not be surprised, for the Lord gives his gifts not for labours, but for humility.'[23] The holy martyr St Maximos said: 'Give your body a little exercise, but put all your efforts on inner work'.[24] St Barsanuphius said: 'If inner godly work does not help a man, his outward labour is in vain'. St Anthony said: 'When I was visiting an abbot, a virgin came and said to the old man: "Abba, I spend my life fasting; I eat once a week and study the Old and New Testaments every day." The old man answered: "Have poverty and plenty become a matter of indifference to you?" "No", she said. "Disgrace and praise?" "No", she said. 'Enemies and friends?" "No", she said. Then the wise old man said: "Go and work, you have achieved nothing." '

Her struggle had been terrific: eating once a week, and surely no delicacies even then, and now suddenly she heard from an experienced staretz: 'You have achieved nothing'. She had studied Holy Scripture too, but had not understood the essence of what it taught, and all her piety was purely

23. *Mystical Treatises*, ch. 58, p. 274.
24. *Four Centuries on Love*, 4,63. *Early Fathers from the Philokalia*, p. 341.

external and did not make her worthy of receiving spiritual fruits. And the five foolish virgins achieved the great, supernatural feat of virginity, but as they had no good deeds (Gal. 5:22) they remained outside the doors to the heavenly palace. And the Pharisees knew Holy Scripture inside out, but they did not live by it, and so could not understand the truth – they crucified the Lord.

Yes, the spiritual life, the science of sciences, requires spiritual judgement which in turn comes from humility. Among the Egyptian startsi if some virtue was disclosed, it was not regarded as a virtue, but a sin. See how the saints feared vanity! The holy archbishop Theophilos visited Mount Nitria and the abbot of the mount said to him, 'According to your knowledge from experience, what is the highest virtue on the monastic path?' The staretz answered: 'Obedience and constant self-reproach'. The archbishop said: 'There is no other path than this'. St Barsanuphius the Great said: 'If you fulfil three conditions, wherever you live you will be at peace. The first is to leave your little will behind you; the second is to reproach yourself; and the third is to regard yourself as worse than everyone else.'

O blessed obedience, whoever bends his head under thy yoke will always have peace and joy. The fruits are comforting, but they do require great labour. The Holy Fathers even compared obedience to martyrdom. Give your blood and receive the spirit. True obedience gives birth to humility, dispassion and even insight – do not be surprised – it is truly so. I shall not write you examples of obedience; I assume that you have read them yourselves and know them.

And here is another thing: in our inattentive living we

do not examine ourselves, but others; and we demand that others should reform while we ourselves remain unreformed – sometimes there is even slander, with its sad consequences. Let me give you an example. This happened in the south in a convent where 400 nuns were working out their salvation. A tailor was passing and met a novice somewhere outside the convent. He said: 'Have you some work for me?' She answered: 'No, we do our own work'. This meeting and exchange of words was seen by another novice, and after some time she had a quarrel with this sister and in the heat of anger she went and slandered her about this meeting. The slandered sister could not endure the disgrace and threw herself into the Nile and drowned. The slanderer, realizing that she had maligned her for nothing and destroyed her, hanged herself. What a sad story. In the same convent God's fool Isidora was working out her salvation, and St Pitirim came to her. When her spiritual exploit was revealed, she, because of her humility, could not bear human fame and secretly left and nobody knows where she lived and how she died. Blessed art thou, Isidora, pray to God for us sinners!

This convent was on the river Nile, and on the other side of the river were ten monasteries with a thousand monks in each. All the monasteries were directed by St Pachomius. Each monastery had an igumen. In the convent the services were celebrated by a priest-monk from the monastery of Pachomius. He forbade prayers for the novices who had perished, and any others who spoke slander he excluded from Communion for seven years. Lord, deliver me from human slander and teach me to do thy will.

And another thing: in the same country and at the same time two brothers, one twelve years old, the other fifteen, were living in a monastery. The igumen sent them to take food to a hermit. They took it and on the way back they encountered a poisonous snake. The younger brother took the snake, wrapped it in his cloak and took it to the monastery, not without conceit, of course. The monks gathered round the boys, were astonished, and praised them as saints. The igumen led a spiritual life and had good sense. He birched the boys and said: 'You took credit for God's miracle. It is better to have an uneasy conscience than virtue with conceit.' For he knew that miracles are harmful to saints.

No, on earth there is no perfection or constancy. There have been cases in which ascetics have been ravished and seen the glory of the saints 'and then fallen and led a shameful life and become a laughing-stock. There was such an ascetic living with St Makarios the Great, and he was so filled with grace that he healed the sick by the laying on of hands, but when he fancied himself to be a saint he was lost, led a shameful life and so ended his days. The holy prophet Ezekiel says that if a righteous man turns away from the path, the Lord will not remember his righteousness, and if a sinner reforms, the Lord will not remember his sins [Ezek. 18].

No, we must not trust ourselves before we are lying in our graves, and whether we persevere in virtue depends not on us, but on the grace of God. The Lord preserves the humble; in so far as a man humbles himself, he flourishes in the spiritual life. Ours it is to labour over self-will, but

96

success depends on grace. So it is that we must pray and ask help from the Lord. The chief work in the spiritual life is prayer, and prayer requires attentiveness and sobriety. I suppose that you have read about prayer. All the same, I will tell you, briefly of course; it is difficult to write in detail about prayer.

Prayer has three degrees: oral prayer, prayer of the mind and mental prayer of the heart. The first, oral prayer, is pronounced with the lips, but the mind strays; in the second, mental prayer, the mind must be enclosed in the words of the prayer. The heart should not be pressed with attention; if attention is on the upper chest, the heart will feel it too. The third, prayer of the mind in the heart, is possessed by very few and is a reward for the deepest humility. A passionate person should not presume to approach this prayer, says St Gregory of Sinai. One should not strive for tender feeling and tears, but when they come of themselves, tenderness and warmth of heart, stop and wait until they have passed. But you must not think that you have received something great. It is a natural result of concentration, but it is no demonic deception either. I will say this too just in case: if the warmth spreads over your whole body, it is not due to the blood; it is spiritual. Then tears begin to pour in streams and people seem simply angelic. At such a moment one's legs no longer hold up, and one has to lie or sit down. If it happens in church you have to go out quickly, because others, not having known or experienced such phenomena in prayer, will think it is demonic deception. It is nothing of the sort, but the visit of a heavenly guest.

Work hard at prayer; the Lord will give prayer to him who prays. Amen.

I have read Hymn VII of St Symeon the New Theologian. It describes the highest level of spiritual contemplation, which is given to man by the grace of God when his heart has been freed of passions. Your dear little mind is too limited to comprehend these hymns. The Holy Fathers write: 'Anyone who aspires to contemplation without having purified his heart of passions incurs the wrath of God'. I advise you not to read the hymns of the Holy Father, for they are not useful to you. Read books on the active life and cleanse your heart of passions. When your heart is freed of passions, then the contemplative level will also be comprehensible to you.

In reading the hymns of the Holy Father you are surprised: 'How was it possible to come to know the inexpressible and write it down?' When by the grace of God a person is illumined from on high through union with the Lord, then the Lord reveals his Divine secrets, and this is incomprehensible to our carnal mind. We may read, but in essence we cannot understand. You advise me to keep this hymn in my heart as a secret. Of course I am unworthy of experiencing in my heart such a high level of contemplation, but all the same, when I read the five-volume *Philokalia* I understand this level as far as my limited mind permits, for it is well explained there, but in another order than in the hymns of St Symeon.

Not so long ago I read a book of Kallistos Kataphygiotes translated from the Greek, about Divine union and the contemplative life. The whole book speaks of contemplation and union with God, like the hymns of St Symeon.

81   *28 April 1954*

The Holy Church sings: 'Let us purify our senses, and we shall see'.[25] Briefly put; but what depth there is in these words. They refer to two states of man: the active and the contemplative. If with God's help a person cleanses his heart from passions: pride, conceit, hypocrisy, slyness, anger and the rest, then by the Lord's grace he comes to the original state in which Adam was created. Yes, this is the state of the holy people of God. Without the active life there can be no contemplative life, and not without purpose were the Holy Fathers up in arms against themselves as against an enemy.

The Holy Fathers went through these two lives, active and contemplative, in experience, and they have left us their legacy in their wise writings. Nor can their writing be understood fully by the mind alone. It is understood through living.

25. Easter canon, first ode.

It is very sad to hear that priests are teaching their spiritual children that when they pray they should make mental pictures of the Saviour or the Mother of God or some saint.

This way of praying is incorrect, even harmful. I know that some who prayed that way have damaged their minds and had to go to doctors for treatment.

I shall tell you briefly how to pray, on the basis of the wise Holy Fathers. The mind should be enclosed in the words of the prayer and attention should be focused on the upper part of the chest, for attentiveness is the soul of prayer. Attention should not be pressed upon the heart; if attention is focused on the chest, the heart will be in sympathy. When tender feeling and warmth of heart appear, do not think you have received something great. This is a natural result of concentration, but it is not demonic deception. All the same, the Lord in his grace gives some consolation to one who prays.

Try with all your might not to condemn anyone for anything. What you do not want done to you, do not do to others. And do not have enmity; otherwise prayer will not be implanted in your heart.

N told me that your mother has died and you are dejected and sorrowing over her. You should not grieve; your mother has not died but moved to the other, eternal world, for the body is of the earth and will go into the earth, but the soul is from God and will go to him. This life of ours is temporal and full of various sorrows, and no one can escape them, only the sorrows are different. But as the soul is created in the image and likeness of God, it will find rest and comfort nowhere but in God. If we establish ourselves in God's will, the sorrows will only trouble us slightly.

Your mother has now been freed from all these earthly sorrows and will live eternally in the other world, which has no end; and the whole race of man, from Adam to the Saviour's Second Coming to earth, will go there.

We must believe strongly in the Gospel and try as far as our strength endures to fulfil the commandments of the Saviour. But we are like deaf people and do not hear the Lord calling us. 'Come to Me all who labour and are heavy laden and I will give you rest' [Matt. 11:28]. He it is who alone can give us rest. Amen.

84   *21 July 1954*

You write that you have read in the Holy Fathers about a disciple who told his staretz that some people are granted to see the holy angels. The staretz replied: 'Blessed are those who constantly see their sins'.

St Peter Damascene writes: 'If you see your sins as sands of the sea, it is a sign of a healthy soul'. You write: 'I cannot understand how saints can see their sins as sands of the sea'. This represents the high degree of spiritual maturity of the men of God, those who with God's help have cleansed their hearts of passions: pride, conceit, slyness, hypocrisy and other vices. However, even they were not free from impacts and suggestions from passions. For as long as the soul is in the body it cannot possibly be freed from these impacts, whether it wants them or not. But when they have overcome the passions within them through virtues, their minds can repel these attacks with God's help. God alone is perfect and unchanging.

Although the Holy Fathers by God's mercy prospered in the spiritual life, they were subject to changes. Sin continued to use cunning; they even had impure and bestial thoughts. Do not be surprised at this, it is so. I am not writing this as my own wisdom; these are the thoughts of men of godly wisdom. These changes in their pure hearts make them see their sins 'as the sands of the sea', and they genuinely regard themselves as worse than anyone else.

We sinners in our careless way of living sometimes say that we are sinful and even that there is none in all the world like ourself. But this is only idle talk and mere words. If we were speaking from the feelings of our heart, we would not have been condemning others for anything, nor been proud, angry, and so on. We ourselves do not keep a single commandment, but we expect others to do so. Oh, the blindness of our hearts! Lord, grant that I may see my sins and not judge my brother.

No doubt you have now understood the deep thoughts of the holy men of God. I ask your holy prayers.

Realize that in the Second Coming of our Lord Jesus Christ
the Dread Judgement will be according to the Holy Gospel.
Yet we have become so earthly-minded that we pay little
attention to the Gospel commandments, while we judge
very severely on any matter of ritual. Of course we must
carry out the rites established by the Holy Fathers, for they
educate our souls in piety. But all the same, we must always
give greater attention to the Gospel commandments. The
Lord says: 'Judge not, that you be not judged, do not do
to others what you would not have them do to you' [Matt.
7:1,12]. But we, as if deaf, do not hear what the Lord says
to us and we freely break his holy commandments.

He who condemns is always in error and judges wrongly,
for we do not know the reason for a sin, but we judge
according to our own temperament. A man draws conclu-
sions about other people in line with his own tendencies,
for a crooked eye looks at everything in a crooked way. St
Dorotheos said very well: 'If a man stands at the corner of
a building and three people pass him, each one thinks
about him in his own way. A religious man thinks: "He is
probably going to church and is waiting for the bells to
ring". A thief thinks: "When it gets darker he will go and
steal". And a fornicator thinks: "He is surely waiting for
a woman to sin with" '. Very rightly said, and we can see
it at almost every step.

I shall give you one example of how grave a sin it is to
condemn. In a certain monastery a monk fell into fornication. A great staretz said: 'What a bad thing he did'. The

monk died and an angel at God's command brought his soul to the staretz and said: 'Where do you want to assign this monk: to Heaven or torment?' The staretz was horrified; he understood what a grave sin condemnation was, and he wept bitterly. After some time the angel said: 'God has forgiven your sin'. However, the staretz did not stop weeping as long as he lived.

Remember us, Lord, when Thou comest into thy Kingdom.

86   *4 August 1954*

I shall answer your long letter briefly.

You write that for twenty-five years you have been reading and listening and feeding on God's word, but it was no use. What use do you want it to have? Or do you want to see yourself faultless and holy in everything? This does not happen in the spiritual life. Be satisfied with seeing your inadequacies, for from this gradually, imperceptibly comes humility, if only to a small degree. And our deviations and attractions to worldly allurements are very humbling to our ego. I recall having written to you about this more than once.

It is good that you and N want to take up prayer. Good wishes, the Lord give you wisdom! However, realize that every good deed: spiritual conversation, reading of soul–saving books, tolerating injury and so on, all belong to prayer.

The Lord in his mercy help you to make a good beginning.

5 August 1954

Christ is in our midst!

. . . You ask me to give you instructions or set up a rule for you and put your life on the true path. This request of yours exceeds my understanding and my spiritual capacity, but for the sake of obedience, forgetting my weakness and inability, I write what the Lord lays on my heart.

Try not to condemn anyone for anything. Whatever you do not want done to you, do not do to others either. Remember that for each idle word we are to answer before God at the Dread Judgement. One cannot serve two masters. Be reconciled with your adversary, lest he put you into prison [Matt. 5:25]. Beware of enmity with anyone, otherwise your prayer will not be pleasing to God, but will even count as sin. How will God forgive our sins when we ourselves do not forgive?

These are the basic instructions on which our salvation is founded. Of course it is easy to say and easy to wish, but to carry it out is very difficult, and we are weak. Our powers alone are not enough – we have to ask God's help, that in his mercy He would help us sinners. Thus the Holy Fathers chose the Jesus Prayer – unceasingly. For you, living in the world, it is very difficult to maintain unceasing prayer, but realize that the Holy Fathers counted every good deed as prayer: good conversation, remembrance of

God, patience in the face of slander, reproach, scorn, ridicule, and so on.

You want to have a definite rule of prayer. St Isaac the Syrian advises us not to burden ourselves with a great number of psalms to be read and thus to be slaves to the rule. For there is no peace in a slavish reading. (Chapter 30 [53], page 136 [256f.] 'On how to pray without whirling thoughts').

In the morning and evening you can read a few prayers; decide for yourself how many, to fit with the time available. But do not waste it in inattention, for attention is the soul of prayer. Every day you should read a chapter of the Gospel and a chapter of the Epistles.

I have written what was on my heart by God's mercy; take it not as a law or command but as advice. See for yourself what fits with the conditions of your life.

88   *21 August 1954*

You are troubled that some of the clergy perform the service very carelessly, and sometimes you do not even feel like going to church. Realize and believe firmly that the Holy Mysteries take place not according to the worthiness of the priests, but by the mercy and grace of God's love.

Here is a graphic example for you: a certain hermit used to be visited by a presbyter from the nearest church and given Holy Communion. Somebody slandered the presbyter to the hermit and the hermit refused to receive him. The presbyter went away. And then the hermit heard a voice: 'Men have usurped My judgement'. After this the hermit fell into a trance and had a vision. He saw a golden well, a gold bucket and a golden rope, and the water in the well was of especially good quality. He saw a leper at the well drawing water and filling a vessel. The hermit could not drink because it was a leper who was drawing water. And again he heard a voice: 'Why do you not drink the water? What is it to you who draws from it? He is only drawing it and pouring it into a vessel.' The hermit came to himself, summoned the presbyter and asked him to give him Holy Communion as before (*Paterikon*).

Never condemn priests; they commit sins and they too will answer to God on the day of judgement. Rather pray for them and inwardly ask for their holy prayers. So the Holy Fathers teach. You see the inadequacies of priests, but look at yourself, how you stand and pray. Why, sometimes the whole service goes by while you are imagining things of this world!

Lord, grant me to see my own sins and not to judge the priests.

89   *21 August 1954*

. . . You ask me: 'Why did the Lord choose Judas the betrayer and call him to apostleship? He knew that he would betray him.' Our little minds are very limited, and we sinners cannot comprehend God's judgements. Five apostles turned away from the Lord. Of course the Lord knows and foresees everything, and in his mercy He calls everyone to Himself. Yet he does not infringe the free will which He has given to us. The Lord gave us commandments to guide us so that we might receive eternal bliss in the coming life, and we are free to fulfil them or not, depending on our will. The Lord has sometimes saved a few by his special Providence: the Apostle Paul, St Mary of Egypt and others. This is an act of God's grace. To us sinners the Lord's dispensations are inscrutable and we must not pry into them, indeed it serves no useful purpose to do so. The best thing is to walk the common path: that of fulfilling the commandments of Christ. Amen.

90 *28 August 1954*

You think so foolishly. You write that there is no God, man dies and everything ends with that, there is no life beyond the grave, it is only man's invention.

In his day the prophet David said: 'The fool says in his heart, "There is no God" ' [Ps. 14.1], and here you have joined yourself to this foolishness. You think so flippantly, but I believe deeply and am convinced that God exists, there is a future life, there is eternal torment for sinners and eternal bliss for the righteous.

How could I not believe in God when wherever I look, everywhere I see and contemplate God's wisdom and goodness. With what wisdom everything is created, and how harmonious is the whole earthly sphere! The Holy Church sings: 'How magnificent are thy works, O Lord; Thou hast made all things in wisdom'.[26] Thy works are marvellous, Lord; wherever I look, everywhere I see thy creative hand. I look at the sun and see it shedding light like a golden plate and warming the whole globe. And what numbers of animals abound in the forest, each with its own characteristics. The horse is so large and yet it obeys man; the Lord created it to help man. And the cow eats hay and its stomach makes nourishing milk for man. And the meek lamb, how much good it does for man; we get fur coats, stockings and much else. I look at the bird kingdom – simply marvellous, how decorative they are and what a variety of species. And in the earth what a variety of worms and insects; there are even worms that shine at night like lights. I look at the ant and wonder at its labours – it exposes my laziness. And the wise bee gathers such sweet honey for man from the different flowers. And look in the water; there is the special kingdom of fish, how many different species; all live and move according to God's purpose.

I love nature altogether. I come into the forest and wonder at every tree and knoll and I contemplate the Almighty Creator. Now I am thinking and wondering at how I came to appear in God's world. My conception was like this: my father's seed fell on my mother's ground in the form of a worm and grew in my mother's womb for nine months and I gradually came into the form of a man. At the end of the ninth month according to the law of nature I came as if out of prison into the wide world. I received an Orthodox

26. Psalm 104, sung at the beginning of Vespers.

baptism; I thank God that I am Orthodox. I believe with certitude in God, in the Holy Trinity, and I believe in Mary the Virgin Mother of God and in all the saints extolled by the Orthodox Church. I believe in the Ecumenical Councils and the whole of Holy Scripture according to the catechism; I believe in everything that our Holy Orthodox Church teaches us.

But this is sad: our Orthodox do not all know their Orthodox teaching; they waver and some even fall into various sects and schisms. They do not know, poor creatures, that all heresies and sects are based on pride and self-suggestion; they say 'we are saved'. They do not recognize the whole Bible but select only what justifies their teaching. One sectarian told me that they know the whole Bible inside out. But I am not surprised at this knowledge of theirs: the Pharisees too knew the whole Bible, but they did not live by it and did not recognize the Truth; they crucified the Lord.

Again I am wondering at God's wisdom. I love the moonlit nights of winter, everywhere utter silence; I put on my fur coat, felt boots and warm cap, go out into the yard and marvel at God's wisdom – the moon is shining, and so many stars, the whole sky is adorned with them, far away and still farther, just single little stars, endlessly. Marvellous are thy works, O Lord, in wisdom Thou hast made them all!

The more I look at nature, the more I wonder at and come to know the omnipotence of the Creator. I was not educated; I have not even read scientific books; I have written this from my feelings, having read the Bible a great deal. My life has passed; I am already in my eighty-second year.

According to the word of the Holy Spirit, man's life on earth is seventy years. Of course many die without reaching that age, but it is an average number. If a man is vigorous he may live eighty years, with difficulties and illnesses after that. Death is an immutable law; the whole race of man from Adam to the Second Coming will pass into another world, and their bodies, at God's command, will rise again. Even those bodies which have been burnt will also rise again; I have no doubt of this. With God everything is possible. Even this beautiful world will in time be done away with, as is said in Holy Scripture.

Mankind has become so earthbound! People have quite forgotten that this life of ours is the path to eternity and a preparation for it: they get excited and worked up in this vale of tears. You meet very few with whom you can even talk about the one thing needful.

91   *30 August 1954*

Christ is in our midst!

. . . You write that even living in a cell one can still sin, one can go on being allured and distracted by the world. This is of course true, and there are many examples which could be cited. Basically monasticism is solitude. The world for lay people and monasticism for monks; everything should be in its own place. In our time the monastic life has started flowing in a different channel. In old Valamo the schema-monks lived apart and had no practical work but only came to the church services and prayed in their cells as each was able. But now the schema[27] does not prevent me from going to work and travelling in towns. And if in my human weakness I happen to stumble, spiritual reason is not surprised. St John of the Ladder says: 'Do not be surprised that you fall every day; do not give up, but stand your ground courageously. Assuredly the angel who guards you will honour your patience' [5,30]. I quoted this saying of the Holy Father so that we should not be depressed if we wavered in some virtue. God is wonderful in his saints.

92   *10 October 1954*

. . . I am alive and sometimes groaning. Because of a bad heart my legs swell, but still I serve. I am preparing to take my week of service; my turn is two weeks from now.

Poor man: in his youth passions torment him, and in old age, infirmities. My life has passed, the passage to another, better world is approaching, where there is neither sorrowing nor sighing. However, it is rather frightening to die; after all, it is something that has never happened to us before. Everyone is afraid of death, says John of the Ladder [6,3].

Our monastic life still has a little glimmer, but our brotherhood has grown old. With God's help the summer work in the fields finished successfully. Even though it was

27. A monastic habit worn by monks of the strict rule.

a rather cold summer, they managed well, better even than the local people. Although the monks are old, they are used to hard work.

So, N, I shall no longer have a chance to sit with you at table and talk with you over a cup of tea about the one thing needful. Yet I hope that we shall meet in the life to come. You are striving to fulfil the commandments of the Gospel; so am I. Let us confess and repent of our frailties as human beings, and the Lord in his mercy will grant us to meet in the life to come. When the devil brings despairing thoughts, drive him away with the whip of prayer, for he is very brazen; he strongly attacks those who aspire to the spiritual life. The holy men of God have experienced such horrors that they did not even want to commit them to writing. However, his evil will is limited; he tempts us as far as the Lord permits, suggesting various thoughts, but our free will can accept them or not, of course, with God's help.

93   *11 November 1954*

. . . Oh, how foolish you are! You write to me that you ' do not believe in God or his holy Providence or in the existence of demons'. Are you really so spiritually blind that you do not see in creation the Creator – Almighty God! Everything is so marvellously made and each thing is regulated by its own law, unchanging from age to age. I remember having written to you about God and his works.

About the existence of demons, I will tell you briefly my

own experience. I was living alone in a little hut in the skete of the Forerunner[28] at Valamo. I prepared my own food; I grew vegetables, but I brought bread from the monastery or once in a while did my own baking. I liked to spend the nights awake. I always lay down after twelve for two or three hours. Of course I slept in the daytime as much as nature required. Once at two o'clock in the morning I was heating the little samovar and instead of supper I was about to drink tea. Suddenly I heard someone walking in the hall; human footsteps could be heard clearly. I remembered well that the doors were locked. My flesh was creeping, and the cat arched its back and its fur stood on end just as if it expected someone to open the door and come in. I took a lamp. went out to the hall, looked everywhere, and there was no one. Of course an unbeliever would say that it was a hallucination. No, it was no hallucination, but demons. Sometimes I heard knockings on the window-frame when I was reading my rule of prayer, and there were other knockings, but I will not describe them all.

Here is some more evidence of the existence of demons, of which the Gospel speaks too. I had a brother living in Petrograd. He kept an eating-house which did a thriving business and I was living in the same city at the time at the Valamo monastery house. Once my brother came to see me. When he came into the cell, for some reason he began to get very agitated. I seated him on a chair, and above it were icons with relics. Suddenly my brother

28. John the Baptist.

114

jumped up from the chair and cried: 'Vile, vile icons!' and
ran out of the cell. I was left at a loss, wondering what had
happened to him. Could he possibly be possessed? It turned
out that he really was possessed. The following day I went
to see him and his wife said to me: 'When he came home
he was very disturbed and began to shout: "I shall never
again go to my brother's; he has vile icons there." And
when I say anything from the Holy Gospel he gets nervous
and says, "Don't say that to me." If the food is sprinkled
with holy water he won't eat it, even if he hasn't seen that
it was sprinkled.' I had to go to the monastery to be consecrated a monk. I arrived at the monastery and asked the
Igumen to remember sick John in the liturgy – he too was
called John; I also asked some schema-monks to pray for
him.

The sacrament took place and I was tonsured. I went
back to the seditious world. I took with me a basket of
strawberries from the monastery garden and sprinkled
them with holy water, thinking to give my brother monastery berries as a treat. I arrived in town, took the berries
and went to give them to my brother. I watched; he ate
and thanked me for the good berries. Then he said to me:
'When you had left for the monastery, in the night I had
just begun to fall asleep when suddenly I saw very clearly
two schema-monks coming towards me and saying to me
kindly: "Do not be sad, do not be sad, you will get well,"
and they left me. I was all right immediately.' Then he
said: 'Bad people had corrupted me out of envy.'

I shall never forget that happening. I believe in God and
in his power and in his marvellous creation. Wherever I

look, everything amazes me and I feel his creative care for the destinies of the world and man.

How is it that you atheists cannot recognize God the Creator when you look at all this wonderful creation? The Lord in his grace marvellously created everything, He gave each thing its appointed law and upholds the order of his world until his Second Coming. Then this marvellous world will be done away with and there will be eternal life which has no end.

94 *18 January 1955*

N's question whether he should decide to go the old way or start a new one is enigmatic: what are these ways? However, I suppose he should go the old way, because he knows it and has experience, but on the new way there is no knowing what he may be faced with. He points to the ascetics: they broke off their life, abandoned everything and changed their life. The ascetics had one aim – to save their souls, and they had a deep faith in God's help. But N has material interests; there is a great difference between them. N understands humility in its external aspect, and so he says: How far should it go? True humility should go so far that a person feels clearly in his heart that he is worse than all other men on the whole terrestial globe – worse even than the beasts. The Holy Fathers said: 'Humility is Divine; it bowed the heavens and came down to earth, took our flesh and became the God-man'. You probably cannot understand this; the question is a philosophical one, but the answer is theological. In the choice of a way one must be guided by Holy Scripture and not by instinct.

95   *20 January 1955*

. . . I have barely managed to get down to writing to you. Old age interferes – I was in hospital eleven days. They helped me greatly, for the Lord heals through doctors: the Lord created the physician, says Holy Scripture. When you address your prayer to the Saviour or the Mother of God or some saint, all these denizens of heaven hear you – have no doubt of this. Pray like this: do not make any sensory representations in your mind of the Saviour, the Mother of God, or the saints, but you should keep your mind in the words of the prayer, and your attention on the upper part of your chest. I repeat: let your attention descend from your head to the verbal region of your chest. As I said above, that is the best way to pray, and may you always use it. Of course it will be difficult at first to descend from your head to your chest, but then your attention will no longer be difficult to keep in your chest. It would be good to have a personal conversation about this. Write to me what you do not understand about prayer and I shall explain.

I wish you peace, love and concord from the Lord.

96   *6 February 1955*

. . . I like to read the sayings of the Holy Fathers, for they spoke 'much sense in short words'.

A certain staretz said: 'If the soul has only words but no deeds, it is like a tree which has blossoms but no fruit'.

You are wonderful, staretz; how well you explained the spiritual life in short words. Flowers only attract the eye: when you leave them you forget them; but the fruit of the tree satisfies a man's hunger and gives strength to support his life. It is the same with those who speak: when they 'speak from deeds', their words fall on the heart like plaster on a wound. But if a person speaks from instruction, one feels that his words are only in his head. Water and vinegar are the same colour, but the throat knows which to drink.

97 *6 February 1955*

In the Gospel of Matthew [16:18] the Lord says: 'You are Peter [the rock] and on this rock I will build my Church, and the gates of hell shall not prevail against it'.

For the word of God is unchanging from age to age. How the pagans and atheists persecuted God's Church! Nevertheless the Divine service always took place and will take place until the Second Coming of our Lord Jesus Christ. The Holy Fathers advise us to read the Holy Gospel every day. If you have very little leisure, read one lesson anyway. Read not just for the sake of getting it read, but pray inwardly to the Lord to open the eyes of your heart to understand the power of Christ's good news; read attentively, as if you were spelling it out. You will learn from experience the spiritual power that comes from such reading – like to the woman with an issue of blood.

I received your letter. You write that sometimes during prayer you are very much disturbed by blasphemous thoughts; they are so shabby that one is somehow ashamed even to look at the icons or to speak to the priest. Do not be embarrassed, for such thoughts are not ours but those of the enemy of mankind – the devil. Simply do not pay attention to them, and try to turn your thoughts to some external objects. This devil is a blasphemer. Sometimes during the Divine Liturgy he blasphemes the Lord, the Holy Mysteries and all that is Divine. St Nicetas Stethatos said: 'That blasphemer, the devil, sometimes by our mouths reviles us and the God Most High'.

St John of Karpathos said: 'Not only before the end of the world will the devil speak words against the Most High, as Daniel says [7:25], but he does so even now, through our thoughts'. We send grievous blasphemies to heaven itself and revile the Most High, and his creation, and the Holy Mysteries of Christ. That blasphemer, the devil, tempted our Lord Jesus Christ with gluttony, vanity and pride. The devil did not know the secret of the Incarnation of the God-man, and yet for some reason he conjectured: 'If you are the Son of God', and the rest, as it tells in the Gospel [Matt. 4:3–9]. The Lord said: 'Begone from me, Satan!' So you tell the blasphemer, the devil: 'Begone from me, Satan, I know our Lord Jesus Christ, I listen to Him and obey Him in everything that is commanded in the Holy Gospel, and whatever you may say, I will not listen to you, who are lost for ever because of your pride: begone from me, you hater of all good'.

Although the devil blasphemer tempts everyone, the proud suffer more from blasphemous thoughts, for the Lord permits the devil to tempt a man because of his pride. The Holy Fathers experienced such blaspheming that they did not even want to commit it to writing. But they were experienced in the spiritual life and were not confused, for they knew well that the perpetrator of blasphemy is the devil.

99   *15 March 1955*

St Ephraim the Syrian prayed: 'Yea, O Lord and King, grant me to see my own sins and not to judge my brother'.[29]

The great Father knew very well and remembered the gravity of the sin of judging and the great virtue of not judging. The Lord said: 'Judge not, that you be not judged. For with the judgement you pronounce you will be judged. Why do you see the speck that is in your brother's eye, but do not notice the log that is in your own eye?' [Matt. 7:1–4]. He who judges others is like Antichrist, for he usurps the judgement of God. Examples of judging others are plentiful.

I shall give you one example of how great a sin it is to judge. St Isaac of Thebes, on a visit to a coenobium,[30] saw

29. *A Manual of Eastern Orthodox Prayers*, p. 38.
30. Community of hermits who occupy separate cells within a common enclosure.

there a brother who had fallen into sin, and he condemned him. When he returned to his cell, an angel stood in his way and said: 'God has sent me and told me to ask you where you order this fallen brother whom you have condemned to be put'. The staretz was horrified and realized the gravity of the sin of condemning. He fell at the angel's feet and in tears asked forgiveness. The angel said: 'God has forgiven you, but beware of judging anyone before God has done so'.

We sinners are so used to judging others. It has become a real habit, and we do not remember God's injunction and the gravity of this sin.

Our judgement is always erroneous, for we do not know the reasons which prompted the sinner to act that way. We see only the sin of our neighbour, but not his repentance. Lord, grant me to see my own sins and not to judge my brother.

100   *24 March 1955*

. . . Tomorrow is the Great Feast of the Annunciation (the good news) to the Ever-Virgin Mary by the Archangel Gabriel. Wonder of wonders! The uncontainable God and Creator of the whole universe is contained in the womb of the Virgin Mary. Most Holy Mother of God, save us sinners! Oh! How well our Holy Church praises the Ever-Virgin Mary in the hymns. We should always listen attentively to these hymns, for they sing of the Old Testament prototypes of the Virgin Mary. May the Lord and the

Queen of Heaven help you in your difficult moments. Believe and turn to them for help.

101   *20 April 1955*

I received your letter and you asked me to write to you about the Incarnation of the Son of God. I have long been thinking of writing this for myself as a reminder, but I somehow could not get started, and now you have given me the impetus.

I venture to enter upon this great task and my soul trembles: how can I write about such a great Secret? Even the holy angels cannot comprehend this great Mystery. Yet, with God's help, I shall write, as far as a man with his limited little mind can grasp this Great Secret of the Incarnation of God the Word. I base my writing on the Holy Church and the teaching of the Holy Fathers, not on my own philosophizing. But my heart trembles: how can the Holy Trinity be consubstantial and undivided; how is the Son of God, who cannot be comprehended, contained in the human womb of the Ever-Virgin Mary; and how did He receive from her a soul and a human body and become perfect God and perfect man, without sin; how did He have the will of God and of man, though his human will was surrendered to God's will? My heart trembles: how can I go on writing about such a mystery?

God is invisible and incomprehensible; even the angels cannot gaze upon Him. But the Lord in his mercy comes down to mankind by his Incarnation. Oh, miracle of miracles! God uncontainable was contained in the womb of the Ever-Virgin, and according to the law of human nature was carried for nine months in the womb of the Ever-Virgin Mary and was born as man, but his birth was painless, for the conception was not of the flesh but from the Holy Spirit. And the Divine Child was laid in a manger and fed with his mother's milk as a human being. 'And the child grew and was strengthened by the Spirit, being filled with wisdom, and the grace of God was upon him.' Oh, what a great marvel: He lived, was brought up and obeyed the holy Joseph until the age of thirty and worked at the carpenter's trade. He sawed, hewed, planed and in general did the work of a carpenter. As a twelve-year-old boy in Jerusalem in the Hebrew synagogue He astonished the Pharisees with his questions and answers, and nothing more is known until He is thirty years old, for God concealed his own Divinity. Oh, the depth of Divine wisdom and humility!

When He was thirty He was led up by the Holy Spirit into the desert and lived there with the wild animals. As a man He endured hunger for forty days and was tempted by the devil [Matt. ch. 4]. He went about teaching mankind as it pleased Him for three and a half years. He acted as God and as man. When He was in a boat with his disciples He slept in the stern like a man; a storm arose and their boat began to fill up. His disciples in fright awakened Him: 'Master, we are perishing' [Luke 8:24]. The Lord rebuked the waves and the wind – as God. When the Lord came to the grave of the dead Lazarus, He wept as a man, but He raised him as God, saying to him who already stank of

123

death: 'Lazarus, come out' [John 11:43]. As a man He walked, got tired, drank, ate and wept as men do, but as God He performed miracles, healed the sick, raised the dead. The learned Pharisees knew Holy Scripture inside out, but they did not live according to the law and could not understand the holy truth. They persecuted the Saviour of the world at every step and carried their animosity so far as to crucify the Lord.

Marvellous are thy works, O Lord. As a man You endured all kinds of abuses from the evil Pharisees. They said: 'He heals the sick, raises the dead and performs other miracles by the power of the demons'. And the Lord for our salvation endured all this as a man. Wonderful is the humility of the Son of Man. He rode on an ass as a man and at his festive entry into Jerusalem the people spread their garments on the road and with loud rejoicing shouted: 'Blessed is the King who comes in the name of the Lord: peace in heaven and glory in the highest' [Luke 19:38]. After the festive entry into Jerusalem the Lord at the Last Supper instituted the sacrament of Holy Communion, and even Judas received Communion of the Body and Blood of the Saviour, our Lord Jesus Christ.

The Lord as a man grieved and mourned: 'My soul is very sorrowful, even to death' [Mark 14:34] and he prayed, saying: 'My Father, if it is possible, remove this cup from me; yet not what I will but what Thou wilt' [Luke 22:44]. And his sweat was like drops of blood falling to the ground. And as a man He suffered insult, derision, blows on the cheeks, and being struck on the head with a stick. And they put a crown of thorns on his head, and blood poured over his clothing and they mocked Him and said: 'Hail, King of the Jews' [Matt. 27:30]. And the wicked Pharisees led the Lord – the Creator of the whole universe and all creatures – to his crucifixion. They nailed his all-pure Body to the Cross. Lord, forgive my impiety in daring to describe thy honourable sufferings. I write not in learned language, for I have not been through school, but as I felt so I have written. I copy the following from the book *Sacred History.*

Crucifixion was a most horrible execution. It included everything that is agonizing in tortures and death: giddiness, cramp, exhaustion of powers, feverishness, being stunned, gangrene in the wounds – all this together and in the highest degree, and without loss of consciousness. The nailing to the cross in a hanging position made the slightest movement agonizing, and the burning, swollen and ever widening wounds from the nails were attacked by gangrene. The veins, particularly in the head and body, were strained from the rush of blood and burst. To all these tortures were added the unendurable heat and unquenchable thirst. All these tortures produced such unbearable pain that those being crucified entreated as the greatest mercy that their lives be ended. Lord, have mercy! And all these horrible sufferings our Lord Jesus Christ endured as a man for our salvation, and the Divinity in Him suffered too. Oh wonder of wonders! Man, does not your hardened heart shudder when you recall these sufferings of Jesus Christ?

Now, as you wished, I have written briefly to you. I advise you to read the Holy Gospel every day. If you do not have time for a whole chapter, read even a few verses.

I received your letter and understood it all. However, do
not be depressed or grieved that you shouted at N – it is
human. Besides, it is humbling and helps you to know your
own state. See what weaklings we are – a contrary wind
blows, and patience is exhausted. To live together and get
on well with each other is very difficult, for temperaments
and characters differ and in order to have peace there must
be efforts towards peace on both sides.

I read in the *Paterikon*: two startsi lived together. At the
beginning one said to the other: 'How do I look to you?'
The other answered: 'Like an angel'. After they had lived
together for some time he asked again: 'And now how do
I look to you?' The other answered: 'Now you look like the
devil and every word of yours sticks into me like a nail'. I
have quoted this example not to indulge you, but so that
you should not be depressed when something happens
because of our weakness.

St Moses said: 'Strength, for one who desires to acquire
the virtues, consists in not losing heart when he chances to
fall, but in continuing again on his way: not to fall is
characteristic only of angels'.

On thoughts

Thoughts are of three kinds: human, angelic and demonic.
Human thoughts are nothing other than fanciful images of

things of this world,, said St Hesychios. Angelic thoughts are always good ones and there is peace and stillness and even a kind of joy in the heart. Demonic thoughts are always sinful and there is a sense of confusion in the heart. At times some people say: 'Take a step and you sin'. It is wrong to say that. In the Holy Fathers all thoughts that come are called suggestions; even if they are bad they are sinless. By our own will we can either accept them or not. If we do not accept them, they are sinless; but if we accept them and enter into converse with them, then they become sinful and will lead to bodily sin. Sometimes unpleasant thoughts come: in the past mistakes have been made, and suddenly they appear like a flash of lightning. I suspect that such thoughts are natural human recollections of the past. But demonic thoughts are always sinful: they have to do with anger, fornication, love of money, conceit, pride and other passions, and the heart is always confused. Of course it is difficult, even impossible for the layman to distinguish the causes of thoughts. For some thoughts are writers' thoughts, some are inventors', and some merchants' thoughts.

104   *6 August 1955*

I received your letter and am writing immediately. In all perplexing questions take as a rule for yourself the advice of the Holy Fathers: if you are faced with two evils, choose the lesser; and if you are faced with two virtues, choose the greater. Of course, pray first that the Lord should give you understanding.

105

I thank you very much for the watermelon, although the package arrived in battered condition, the watermelon damaged, the paper all wet. The postmistress was displeased; other packages got wet. No doubt you sent it with vanity. It always happens that anyone who acts with vanity can expect disgrace.

106

Christ is in our midst!

I am glad you remember Valamo and that you feel helped by Sts Sergei and Herman. You write that you have been on bad terms with your aunt now for sixteen years and you cannot be reconciled. It is very sad. Realize that your virtues are not pleasing to God. How can you read the Lord's Prayer '. . . forgive us our trespasses as we forgive them that trespass against us'? You yourself do not forgive, but ask God's forgiveness? You pray in vain; God will not forgive you until you are reconciled with your aunt. Read the fifth chapter of Matthew, verse 23. The Lord himself even prayed to his Father on behalf of his crucifiers: 'Father, forgive them, for they know not what they do' [Luke 23:34]. And the holy apostle Archdeacon Stephen prayed for those who stoned him: 'Lord, do not hold this sin against them' [Acts 7:60]. See what examples we have – and you cannot be reconciled with your aunt. You write that she offended you, but take a careful look at yourself: perhaps you yourself were not in the right. Even supposing she offended you for no reason, still you should go to her and be reconciled. Although your hard heart does not want to make peace, force it, pray to God and ask his help that the Lord may soften your heart. Do it without fail or you will be lost. For God's judgement in the Second Coming will be by the Gospel.

In the prayer before Communion it says: 'Go and make peace with those who have brought you sorrow'. If you come to Holy Communion without having been reconciled, it will not be Communion.

Here is another case in church history: A priest Saprikios and a layman Nikiphoros were very great friends. The devil put such enmity between them that they could not make peace. At that time the Christians were being persecuted. The priest Saprikios suffered many tortures and was sentenced to be beheaded. Nikiphoros asked the priest: 'Martyr of Christ, forgive me for Christ's sake'. But the hard-hearted priest did not forgive him and said to the torturers: 'I renounce Christ'. Nikiphoros declared himself to be a Christian and they chopped off his head. Saprikios was lost, but Nikiphoros became a martyr. You see what a serious sin hostility is; a man suffered such heavy tortures and then was lost. I have written you just a small example out of many. Write me no more letters until you are reconciled with your aunt.

I ask God's blessing on you; the Lord reconcile and keep you.

107

I received your letter and you ask me to reply. You find the following words in the holy Apostle Paul incomprehensible: 'We know that in everything God works for good with those who love Him, who are called according to his purpose. And those whom He foreknew He also predestined ... And those whom He predestined He also called; and those whom He called He also justified; and those whom He justified He also glorified.' [Rom. 8:28–30].

I answer not by my own wisdom, but on the basis of the teaching of the Holy Fathers. The blessed Theophylactus says: 'So first there is foreknowledge and then predestination. A person becomes called according to his foreknowledge, that is according to his own free will (because otherwise everyone would be saved because all are called), but free will is still necessary. And so, first foreknowledge, and then predestination.'

The Lord calls all, 'Come to me, all who labour and are heavy laden' [Matt. 11:28], but He does not violate the free will given to us. For it depends on good will whether we strive for salvation and await grace, or desire evil and turn away from grace.

Realize, my friend, that our little mind is very limited and our heart is still encumbered with passions and we cannot understand the Divine purpose in Holy Scripture.

There are people who out of ignorance of the meaning of Scripture maintain the preposterous teaching that some are absolutely predestined to salvation and others to destruction; as if our most gracious God wanted anyone to perish.

Once while fasting and praying St Anthony the Great asked God to reveal to him why some die in their youth and others in old age, why some live a pious life and are poor, while others live a wicked life and prosper. He heard a voice: 'Anthony, keep your attention on yourself, and do not pry into the judgements of God; it is not good for you'.

Now can man really comprehend God's judgements? Why some people are blind from birth, others crippled, others idiots, and much else; there is a very great deal that is incomprehensible to us. Heresies, sects and schisms have arisen from wrong understanding of Holy Scripture and are based on pride and self-suggestion. In the Orthodox faith the authorities are the Ecumenical Councils and the teaching of the Holy Fathers.

So, friend, this is how I advise you to read the Holy Bible: first pray to God to open your mind to understand, the Scripture. What you understand try to carry it out, and what you do not understand, let it go. That is the advice of the Holy Fathers. Holy Scripture is not to be read for knowledge, but for the salvation of one's soul. Searching into the incomprehensible is connected with pride.

131

It is characteristic of human nature to fear death. Death entered mankind unnaturally: therefore human nature fears death and flees from it.

St Maximos the Confessor says: there is nothing more frightful than the thought of death or more magnificent than the remembrance of God. See how even such a saint was afraid of death, a man who had his tongue cut out for the sake of Orthodoxy. Many say: 'I am not afraid of death; I am ready to die even now'. This is only idle talk, and when they feel the approach of death, then fear will come.

Father John of Kronstadt wrote his experience from his feelings and not from reason, and so his writing lies on the heart like plaster on a wound. For my sins, it was not granted to me to see him. But I always listen with love when he is spoken of by someone who saw him.

I read your letter. You confess to being very talkative. The Holy Fathers said: One person talks all day and it is accounted as silence, for he speaks for God's sake; another is silent all day and it is accounted as empty talk. Examine your own talkativeness and compare it with the advice of the Holy Fathers!

You write further that you are much occupied with everyday cares, and prayer goes badly. You must finally recognize that you are not a nun and are living in the world. How could you live without cares? You read the Holy Scriptures but do not understand the power of their teaching. For even the Holy Fathers did not live without cares, and their prayer stopped too and they sometimes felt very weak. But they, being experienced in spiritual warfare, did not lose heart in these changes but endured their unpleasant experiences. St John Kolovos was so wrapped in unceasing prayer full of grace that he forgot the baskets that he was to give to the cattle-driver; while on his way to fetch them he forgot what he had gone for. When the same holy man was walking with the cattle-driver along the skete path and the driver made him angry, the holy man fled from him. You see, changes happen even in the saints, yet you want everything to go smoothly for you. Remember how I said to you once in our conversation: 'It is better to have an uneasy conscience than virtue with vanity'.

Here is what the holy men say: 'If you are struggling as you should, do not be proud of your fasting. If you get conceited about it, what use is the fast? It is better for a person to eat meat than to be arrogant and exalt himself.' St Moses said: 'Strength, for a person who desires to acquire virtues, consists in not losing heart when he happens to fall, but in continuing once more on his way. Not to fall is characteristic only of angels.' Pedants who are ignorant of the power of the spiritual life do not like such sayings, for all their piety is in outward conduct. It is very regrettable that, in our inexperience in the spiritual life, we stick to the letter, for the letter kills, and the spirit gives life.

The Lord keep you in his mercy.

A certain wise staretz admonished a brother for being proud, but the brother answered: 'Excuse me, father, I am not proud'. The wise staretz rejoined: 'How could you demonstrate more clearly that you are proud than by saying, "I am not proud"?'

Yes, pride is blind; it does not see itself. Pride is the devil's invention. Its offspring are: anger, slander, irritability, hypocrisy, envy, contradiction, recalcitrance. It strongly insists on its own opinion, has difficulty in submitting to others, cannot stand criticism, but loves to criticize others, throws out words senselessly; it has no patience, is a stranger to love; is insolent to the point of insult, strives for power. The proud suffer very much from blasphemous thoughts. I have written briefly, on the basis of the teaching of the Holy Fathers.

Now I shall tell about humility. O, blessed humility, Thou art divine, for Thou didst bow the heavens and clothe Thyself in humanity and nail the sins of the whole world to the Cross. My soul trembles; how can I say anything about thy greatness?

Here is what men of godly wisdom said about humility: it gives rise to meekness, affability, tender feeling, compassion, quietness, obedience. A humble man is not curious about incomprehensible things, but a proud man wants to investigate the depth of God's dispensations. A humble person does not take credit for his natural endowments and he shuns people's praise. Just as a man dressed in silk clothes jumps aside if tar is spattered on him, so as not to dirty his precious clothing, so also a humble man flees from human glory.

It is characteristic of humility to see one's own sins but to see the good qualities in others. It is characteristic of pride, on the other hand, to see only the good in oneself and only what is bad in others. Here are other features of humility: simplicity, frankness, naturalness. But what humility is and how it is born in the soul no one can explain in words unless a person learns it from experience. It cannot be learnt from words alone.

Once Abba Zosima was speaking about humility and a learned sophist who had listened to him said to the staretz: 'How can you consider yourself a sinner, do you not know that you are holy? Do you not know that you have virtues? Surely you see how you fulfil the commandments, and do you think that you are a sinner?' The staretz did not find anything to say and only replied: 'I do not know what to say to you, but I regard myself as a sinner'. The sophist insisted, wanting to find out how this could be. Then the staretz was again at a loss for words and said in his holy simplicity: 'Do not confuse me; I really regard myself so'. Abba Dorotheos was there too and he explained this to the sophist: 'Just as in the sciences there are certain ways which cannot be explained, so also there are in humility'. Abba Zosima embraced him and said: 'You have understood the matter; it is just as you said'. The sophist was satisfied and agreed with them [Dorotheos, p. 100].

I have put down only a little of the great deal that has been written. If you want to know more and in detail, you can read it in the *Philokalia*.

About dreams

I have heard that many lay people are talking about dreams and making their various conjectures about them. Some of our own respected father-monks believe in dreams and make their interpretations.

On receiving letters from laymen about dreams, some monks, because of their inexperience in the spiritual life read these letters with approval and show them to their brother-monks as something edifying. Such wrong notions about dreams prompted me to make notes from some of the Holy Fathers.

'The demons of vainglory are prophets in dreams. Being sly, they guess the future from present circumstances and foretell it to us. When these visions come true we are amazed; and we are indeed elated with the thought that we are already near to the gift of foreknowledge. A demon is often a prophet to those who believe him, but he is always a liar to those who despise him. Being a spirit, he sees what is happening in the air, and noticing that someone is dying, he foretells it to the more credulous types of people through dreams. But the demons know nothing about the future from foreknowledge, but it is known that even doctors can foretell death. He who believes in dreams is completely inexperienced, but he who distrusts all dreams is a wise man. Therefore he who believes in dreams is like a person running after his own shadow and trying to catch it', (St John of the Ladder on dreams, ch. 3,28). The blessed

Diadochos writes: 'However, let us rather observe as a great virtue the rule not to believe in any dreams. For dreams are for the most part nothing but idols of thoughts, the play of imagination, or again, as I have already said, demonic sneering and mockery of us' [ch. 38].

St Symeon the New Theologian writes: 'Only those can have true visions in sleep (they should not be called dreams but visions), whose mind has been made simple by the grace of the Holy Spirit, and freed from the pressure of passions and from slavery to them. These are men whose only care is things Divine, whose only thought is of future rewards and blessings, whose life is above ordinary life, free of care, not dispersed, serene, pure, full of mercy, wisdom, heavenly knowledge and other good fruits tended in them by the Holy Spirit. In people who are not like this, dreams are disorderly and false, and everything in them is sheer deceit and illusion.'[31]

The wise Sirach writes: 'Vain hopes delude the senseless, and dreams give wings to a fool's fancy. It is like clutching a shadow, or chasing the wind, to take notice of dreams. Divination, omens and dreams are all futile' [Ecclus. 34]. Dreams have led many astray and ruined those who built their hopes on them. There are many examples in the writings of the Fathers, of people perishing through believing in dreams. The Optina staretz priest-monk Leonid said to his pupil: 'One should not believe in dreams even though they may be real in their own way, for many have gone

31. *Writings from the Philokalia on the Prayer of the Heart*, p. 140.

astray through belief in dreams. The philosopher staretz Theosterik, who wrote the canon of consolation to the Most Holy Mother of God, trusted in dreams and finally became so misled that he perished.'

In the *Prologue*[32] there is this story. 'A Mesopotamian monk amazed everyone with his strict ascetic life, but because he began to believe in dreams he perished. He had a dream that the holy Moses and the other prophets and Jews went to Paradise, but the apostles and martyrs, bishops and holy men went to hell. After this dream the monk took the Jewish faith, married a Jewess and began to enter into polemics with the Orthodox.' Many such stories can be told, but these are enough. If God's holy people did have prophetic dreams, like those of the Old Testament Joseph [Gen. 37:5], of Sț Joseph who was betrothed to Mary [Matt. 1:20, 2:13], of the Holy Mother of God, and other saints, it was inwardly announced to them by God. We are told well and clearly in Holy Scripture how to be saved, but our limited and inquisitive little minds are not satisfied with this and want to know something more about the future from dreams. Is it not better for us to be guided by Holy Scripture and the advice of the Holy Fathers than to be carried away by dreams and put our trust in them? Lord, teach us to follow in each and every thing the path of thy commandments.

32. A collection of instructive stories from the lives of the Fathers.

On the Holy Mysteries of Christ

This sacrament, so great, is higher than all the virtues. The
Church sees in it a miracle of the omnipotence of God, like
the creation of the world by God out of nothing. But even
to approach the Holy Communion of Christ's Holy Mysteries we must, as far as it is in our powers, have a pure
conscience, for we are uniting with Christ. And how can
we unite with Christ if we have enmity towards anybody
or look down on them or judge them? The holy Apostle
Paul says: 'For he who eats and drinks unworthily, eats
and drinks judgement upon himself' [1 Cor. 11:29]. At the
beginning of a prayer before Holy Communion it says: 'O
man, that yearn'st to take the Body of the Lord, draw nigh
in fear, lest thou be burnt: it is a fire. And ere thou drinkest
in Communion Blood divine, first go, be reconciled with all
who thee have grieved; then mayst thou courage take to eat
the mystic food.'[33] Do you hear, communicant? Be reconciled – even with him who has grieved you. At the end of
the prayer it says again: 'Tremble, O man, when you see
the deifying Blood, for it is a fire that burns the unworthy'.

Come to Holy Communion in the awareness of your
sinfulness, simply and reverently, aware that you are par-
taking of the very Body and Blood of the Lord. Since we,
because of our bodily nature, cannot taste a body, the Lord
in his mercy has granted us sinners to taste his Body and
Blood in the form of bread and wine.

33. *A Manual of Eastern Orthodox Prayers*, p. 63.

Again your suffering has been repeated. What can you do? It is not without God's will that this happens. If the Lord cares about the birds, can he have forgotten you? Do not stop praying; it will help you.

You write: will the Lord forgive you? This is a thought from the devil; he is frightening you, out of animosity. Do not listen to him. There is no sin which exceeds God's mercy.

The apostle Carpus prayed to the Lord to punish two sinners. A certain heretic had drawn an Orthodox into his heresy, and now the apostle prayed the Lord to punish them. The Lord showed him this vision: the heavens opened; a bright light shone forth. The apostle looked up and saw the Lord. The Lord said to him: 'Now look down'. The apostle looked and saw those two sinners on the edge of a ravine and below was a frightful snake, enormous in size. The Lord said to the apostle: 'Do you want me to punish these sinners?' The apostle was glad that they would be punished. Then the Lord sent two angels to save these sinners and said to the apostle: 'Strike Me and crucify Me a second time: I am still ready to suffer for sinners'. With this the vision ended.

See how great is God's compassion; He is ready again to suffer for sinners, and you are in doubt whether the Lord will forgive you.

I, a sinner, pray to the Lord that in his compassion He may give you patience to bear your sufferings with good heart, without a murmur. I ask your holy prayers.

A certain monk-deacon told me the following: 'On Sunday during the community liturgy after the priest-monk N had received the Holy Mysteries of Christ, his face became radiant like that of St Seraphim of Sarov. I looked at him and could not take my eyes off his face, it was so lovely to look at him.'

This priest-monk has not been outstanding in any way; he lives simply, he is a great worker, takes part in all the work of the monastery and all the services when he is free from work. I will write nothing more about him, a prophet is without honour in his own country.

Glory, Lord, to thy holy condescension towards mankind, for to us sinners Thou givest thy gracious gifts abundantly in all the Mysteries of the Church, but especially at the Divine Liturgy, when we take part in Christ's Holy Mysteries, for here we unite with Christ. We should approach Holy Communion reverently, simply and without affectation, with awareness of our great sinfulness, and not be troubled if sometimes we feel dry and cold. We must not try to have tender feeling, a leaping heart and an illumined face like that of the priest-monk. This is a matter of God's grace, and which gifts He gives when and to whom is according to his own discretion.

The Lord said: 'Ask and it will be given you . . . knock and it will be opened to you' [Matt. 7:7].

I, sinner that I am, got fixed in an old habit, it tormented me for a long time. I fought with it and asked the Lord that I might be freed from it, but the Lord did not help me. I read the Holy Fathers and know in theory the means for combating passions.

The Holy Fathers say that passions begin in this way: an unwanted thought, holding converse with it, being captured by it, and a passion is born. If we cut off the first thought, we will cut off the whole passion with one stroke. But I, in my weakness and laziness, fell captive to passion. I struggled and prayed but could not free myself from captivity. Once it was so painful to me, I confessed my weakness and powerlessness, crying out to the Lord: 'Lord, help me in my weakness to get free of this passion!' and the Lord in his mercy helped me, through people, although they were not aware of doing it, but I clearly felt God's help.

I had prayed previously too, but apparently not sincerely and had trusted more in my own strength than in God's help. Thus the Lord taught me to remember his words: 'Without me you can do nothing'.

Glory, Lord, to thy Holy Compassion.

116   *undated*

Hearty thanks for the icon of St Seraphim. I look at his life and examine my own empty life. It is terrible; sometimes I am ready to tear my hair for my negligence. My lifetime in this vale of tears is nearing its end, and my mortal body, taken from the earth, will be lowered again into the earth. I write these lines and weep, Lord! Help me, faithless sinner that I am, to offer true repentance, like the monk Silouan, whose funeral I performed not long ago, and to whom I gave thy Holy Communion, I who unworthily wear the bright church robes and am called a server and celebrant of the Divine Liturgy, again I weep. I stop writing and lie in bed and go on weeping and the tears flow in streams. Stillness, the fire has gone out, the brothers have gone to bed, and again more tears.

The vain world will go on living its life, and my sinful body will lie in a cold grave. The body was taken from the earth and will return to the earth, says Ecclesiastes [12:7], but the soul will return to God, who gave it. And what have you gained for the age to come? What? The martyrs will show their wounds for Christ, the saints will show their spiritual exploits, but what will you show? You put on the schema and promised in front of the Gospel and the brethren to fight spiritual battles, and how do you live? I go on crying. I have got up, gone and washed, found a candle-end, and I continue writing. I have written to you foolishly, according to my foolishness, but I shall not be foolish, for I wrote my experience, and if you make fun of me – I will not complain about your laughter. But for my chatter – for I am sometimes very talkative – I would like to hang a lock on my mouth, but at present I can't do it; my work as a father-confessor and celebrant prevents . . .

God-loving Father!

I received your letter: you write that your spiritual life is not going well, prayer keeps breaking off, you are attacked by despondency, sloth and dryness and you easily lose hope.

In this temporal life it cannot be otherwise. We have to go through all sorts of adversities like a ship at sea – sometimes winds, sometimes rain, sometimes such a storm that the masts are cracking; sometimes the ship seems about to founder on a reef. At such hard moments it is good to walk in the forest and watch how the squirrels jump from tree to tree and the birds praise the Lord. It is only pitiful man who gets despondent and sad. Another good thing is to talk with someone. But the healers of this painful condition are patience, prayer and time. You are still troubled by old habits and are very depressed. Yes, they are quite distressing experiences, and yet you must not be depressed.

St John of the Ladder says: 'Previous habit often tyrannizes even over him who deplores it. And no wonder! The account of the judgements of God and our falls is shrouded in darkness and it is impossible for the mind to understand it. Do not be surprised that you fall every day; do not give up, but stand your ground courageously. And assuredly the angel who guards you will honour your patience' [5,29–30].

St Moses says: 'Strength for one who desires to acquire the virtues consists in not being faint-hearted when he

144

chances to fall, but in continuing again on his way. Not to fall is characteristic only of angels.'

Here is what St Ephraim the Syrian says: 'The ascetic should know this too: just as the soul is incomparably higher than the body, so the soul's virtues are higher than those of the body, and the vices of the soul are graver and more destructive than those of the body, although I do not know why many intelligent people fail to realize this. They avoid drunkenness, fornication, stealing and vices of this nature, which many fear and are careful to avoid, but they are indifferent about vices far more important, those of the soul: envy, rancour, arrogance, slyness and the root of all evils, love of money.' To some people this may be incomprehensible and hard to take in, but the saint speaks rightly in the way he compares vices of the soul with those of the body. The virtue named for God is love, for God is love.

I wrote this not in order to indulge you, but for your information, for you to have a broader understanding of the spiritual life. Most important, try to be peaceful, and in order to be peaceful do not get involved in matters that do not concern you; avoid talking any sort of nonsense, reading newspapers and looking for news. The Holy Fathers said: 'A monk who leaves his cell is a different man when he comes back'. As for the newspapers and listening to the news, it would be superfluous even to speak about it.

If you are perplexed about anything, write. I shall try to answer as far as the Lord gives understanding to this sinner. I am already eighty-three and I thank God that I have two consolations: first – good eyes so that I can read freely, and

145

secondly – I am able to take care of myself; about my ailments I shall keep silent.

I ask your holy prayers.

BIBLIOGRAPHY

Anthony, St, *Seven Letters of St Anthony*, tr. D. Chitty. Oxford 1975.

Barsanuphius and John, *Questions and Answers*, tr. into French by L. Regnault and P. Lemaire. Solesmes 1972. First part tr. into English by D. Chitty. *Patrologia* Orientalis, vol. xxxi, 3. Paris 1966.

Diadochos of Photike, St, *Oeuvres spirituelles*, ed. E. des Places. *Sources Chrétiennes*, 5, 2nd ed. Paris 1955.

Dorotheos of Gaza, *Discourses and Sayings*, tr. Eric P. Wheeler. Kalamazoo, Michigan 1977.

Early Fathers from the Philokalia, tr. E. Kadloubovsky and G. E. H. Palmer. London 1954.

Gregory of Nyssa, St, *Dogmatic Treatises, etc. Nicene and Post-Nicene Fathers*, Second Series, Vol. v. Oxford 1893.

Isaac the Syrian (of Nineveh), *Mystic Treatises*, tr. A. J. Wensinck. Amsterdam 1923. Recently reprinted.

John Cassian, St, *Works*, tr. Rev. E. C. S. Gibson. *Nicene and Post-Nicene Fathers*, Second Series, Vol. xi, pp. 163–621.

John of the Ladder (Climacus), St, *The Ladder of Divine*

147

Ascent, tr. Archimandrite Lazarus Moore. London 1959.

Macarius the Egyptian, St, *Fifty Spiritual Homilies*, ed. A. J. Mason. London 1921. Recently reprinted in Willets, California.

A Manual of Eastern Orthodox Prayers, Fellowship of Saint Alban and Saint Sergius. London 1945.

Maximus the Confessor, St, *The Ascetic Life. The Four Centuries on Love*, tr. P. Sherwood. London 1955.

Sayings of the Desert Fathers, tr. from Latin by Sister Benedicta Ward. Oxford 1975.

Unseen Warfare, ed. Theophan the Recluse, tr. E. Kadloubovsky and G. E. H. Palmer. London 1952.

Waddell, Helen, *The Desert Fathers*. London 1936.

Writings from the Philokalia on Prayer of the Heart, tr. E. Kadloubovsky and G. E. H. Palmer. London 1951.

The Wit and Wisdom of the Christian Fathers of Egypt, tr. Wallis Budge. Oxford 1934.

SUGGESTED READING

The Art of Prayer, An Orthodox Anthology, comp. Igumen Chariton, tr. E. Kadloubovsky and E. M. Palmer. London 1966.

Brianchaninov, Ignaty, Bishop, *On the Prayer of Jesus*, tr. Father Lazarus Moore. London 1965.

Colliander, Tito, *The Way of the Ascetics*. London 1960.

Dunlop, John B., *Staretz Amvrosy: Model for Dostoevsky's Zossima*. Belmont, Mass. 1972.

Father John of Kronstadt, *Spiritual Counsels*, ed. W. J. Grisbrooke. Cambridge 1967.

Archimandrite Kallistos (Timothy) Ware, *The Power of the Name*. Oxford 1974.

Merton, Thomas, *The Wisdom of the Desert*. London 1973.

'A Monk of the Eastern Church', *The Jesus Prayer. Its Genesis, Development and Practice in the Byzantine-Slavic Religious Tradition*. New York 1967.

— *On the Invocation of the Name of Jesus*. London 1949.

— *Orthodox Spirituality*. London 1945. Reprinted 1978.

Sjögren, Per-Olof, *The Jesus Prayer*, tr. S. Linton. London 1975.

Archimandrite Sofrony, *The Undistorted Image: Staretz Silouan*, tr. R. Edmonds. London 1958.

The Way of a Pilgrim, tr. R. M. French. London 1954.

Zander, Valentine, *St Seraphim of Sarov*. London 1975.

Additional Note (see p. 24): *In the Caucasian Mountains* is a book on the Jesus Prayer by the Schema-priest-monk Ilarion (1907). These pages speak of the presence of Jesus himself in his Name.

INDEX OF THEMES

The numbers given are those of the letters and do not refer to pages.

151